D1591954

PRINCE

CHAPTER AND VERSE

A LIFE IN PHOTOGRAPHS

MOBEEN AZHAR

STERLING
New York

For he who made the world less blue and more purple.

With thanks to Zaeem for introducing me to music and to all the purple people who shared their stories.

A NOTE FROM THE AUTHOR

The paisley-stained label in the center of the twelve-inch single "Gett Off" creates a psychedelic pattern as it spins on my brother's turntable. At the age of eleven, I didn't realize what spell this kaleidoscope was casting or the impact it would have on the rest of my life.

Twenty-two years and a million listening hours later, I dance-walked over to Prince's keyboard. I was on stage with him. What do you do when you're on stage with Prince? Tell him you love him, of course. I did. He looked into my eyes and put his hand over his heart before singing the opening words of "When Doves Cry." Looking at me, he must have known that, in part, I'm a product of his inspiration. The androgynous alien taught me about dance, music, sex, romance. He's in my hair. You can see him on my face and in the way I walk. I would be a different person, perhaps a few shades grayer, if it wasn't for Prince.

His debut was released a year before I was born. I remember wondering where I would be when Prince would release album number 43, 68, or 101. I came to expect that this man would just keep on making music. Like the changing of seasons, there was *always* another Prince album around the corner.

In 2015, I made the documentary *Hunting for Prince's Vault* for the BBC. I visited Paisley Park Studios in Minnesota, where Prince recorded so much of the music that punctuated my life. Meeting Prince's bandmates from every era of his career and reliving the making of so many of his albums was my dream. It planted a seed that became *Prince: Chapter and Verse*.

This is not a biography or an exhaustive history of Prince. It is a collection of conversations I've had with many of Prince's closest collaborators. Those who knew Prince often tell me he lived his life like a movie. The stories I've collected are scenes in this movie that serve to tell us something valuable about him, his creative process, and his perspective.

Mobeen Azhar, 2016

OPPOSITE On stage during the Sign O' the Times tour, Isstadion, Stockholm, May 9, 1987.

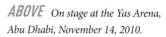
ABOVE *On stage at the Yas Arena, Abu Dhabi, November 14, 2010.*

PREVIOUS PAGE *In front of the Schmitt Music Company building, Minneapolis, 1977.*

CONTENTS

PROLOGUE

Once upon a time, in a land called Minneapolis, lived a Purple Prince. This Afro-crowned boy was the son of a jazz musician and a singer. He had no gold coins, but discipline and talent were his treasure. He taught himself to play piano. He then moved to drums and guitar, playing each with virtuoso skill and making beautiful music all day and all night. When people heard him, they knew this Prince was cool. They lined up around the block to hear him play. The Prince had many masks. He was Jamie Starr, The Kid, Camille, Alexander Nevermind, Joey Coco, Tora Tora, and ♂, too. His voice was like warm honey and ice cream. It took him around the world; singing songs for the rebels and the regal but always coming home to Minneapolis, where he believed the cold and the ice "kept the bad people out."

The fairy tale prose on these pages tell the true story of a magic man. His name has permeated modern music and pop culture for almost four decades. His name is shorthand for airborne guitars, squelchy electro drumbeats, and synths dripped in sex. His name is royal. It's lubricated. It's the deepest purple. His name transcends race, gender, and the confines of the music industry itself. It's as if one little man from Minneapolis is just too big for definition.

There is the pop Prince, the multimillion-selling superstar. There is the ethereal Prince, who sings about making love through the apocalypse, rivers of menstrual blood, and psychedelic masturbation. There is the movie star, the outsider, the pervert, the ghost writer, the live powerhouse, but more than anything, there is the musician: a vessel in which Jimi Hendrix, Little Richard, Joni Mitchell, and James Brown pollinated each other's sounds to create something we'd never heard before.

His name is Prince. He is music.

OPPOSITE *Photo shoot at Kemps Ice Cream building. Minneapolis, 1977.*

THE WHOLE SOUND

IN THE WORDS OF SONNY THOMPSON, BASS, INTERMITTENTLY, 1970–2015

"When he was thirteen he was already a great guitar player and he could really sing. He used to come to my house and borrow pedals for his guitar. We'd compete with what we could come up with. He played me this one song he'd written and it had so many changes in it. They were all so beautiful. I thought, 'Oh my god, man, I'm not playing you my stuff!'

I had my band called the Family. Prince had a band called Grand Central. Jimmy Jam and Terry Lewis had Flyte Tyme. We would play at the same places like the YMCA and the black community center. There was a friendly kind of competition between us all. We all knew the same stuff like Sly and the Family Stone, so we would do the same songs.

He was in my band at one point. I remember in rehearsal he sang and played rhythm guitar on 'Sophisticated Lady,' the Natalie Cole song, and he absolutely killed it. There's a difference between a great keys player, a great singer or whatever, and being an actual musician. That's how he was different. He already knew what the whole sound should be."

OPPOSITE   *Posing during a recording studio at MoonSound studios, Minneapolis, 1977.*

11

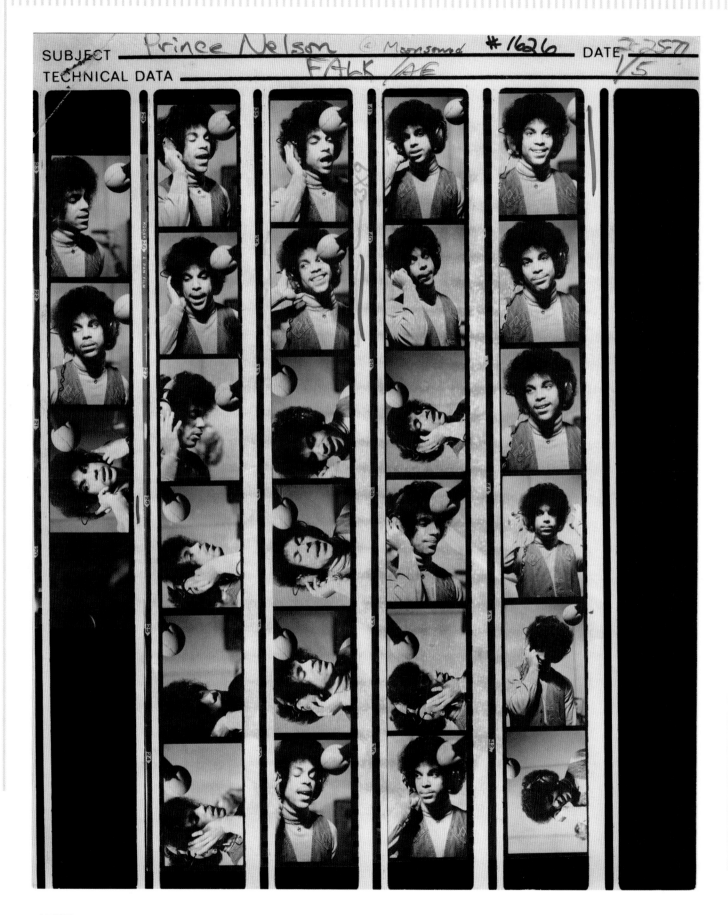

SUBJECT _Prince Nelson_ @ Moonsound #1626 DATE 2-25-77
TECHNICAL DATA _FALK/AE_ 1/5

ABOVE Contact sheet from 1977. Prince is eighteen.

"HE ALREADY KNEW WHAT THE WHOLE SOUND SHOULD BE."

SONNY THOMPSON

ABOVE *Photo shoot at Kemps Ice Cream building,
Minneapolis, 1977.*

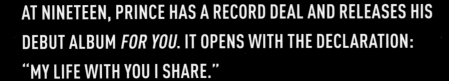

AT NINETEEN, PRINCE HAS A RECORD DEAL AND RELEASES HIS
DEBUT ALBUM *FOR YOU*. IT OPENS WITH THE DECLARATION:
"MY LIFE WITH YOU I SHARE."

A PREVAILING THEME

IN THE WORDS OF GAYLE CHAPMAN, KEYBOARDS, 1978–1980

" I used to jam with Prince's cousin, Charles. He told me to listen to *For You*. I was alone at home with it cranked up too loud and I heard a voice in my head say, 'He'll need a touring band.' I asked around and it turned out Prince was looking.

My audition was in the basement at Prince's house. I walked in wearing a blue-jean tent dress. I was a granola queen. Bobby was on drums. André was on bass. Prince had an Afro that made him just a little shorter than me. There was a Fender Rhodes keyboard down there and Prince asked me to join in.

Three months later, I'm taking a nap and my phone rings. A monotone voice says, 'Hello Gayle, this is Prince. Can you make it to practice in an hour?' I said, 'Sure.' I must have driven at 100 miles an hour. I turned up with my amp in my arms and karate-kicked the door open. Prince looked at me as if to say, 'I hired this nut?' He sat me up in front of an Oberheim and said, 'I've set it the way I want it. Just play.' I was very willing to learn.

There was a lot of experimentation. Above the basement there was an empty living room with just a couch and two chairs. I remember him videoing a woman modeling in a leather jacket with her breasts hanging out. He was working out how things came across on screen and starting to blur the line between his reality and his fantasy. Sex was a side project for him. A prevailing theme. "

RIGHT Studio session at MoonSound Studios,
Minneapolis, 1977.

"HE COULD HEAR MUSIC IN HIS HEAD AND IT WOULD FLOW THROUGH HIS FINGERS." DR. FINK

SOMETHING SPECIAL

IN THE WORDS OF DR. FINK, KEYBOARDS, 1978–1991

"As soon as I joined the group, I knew it was going to be something special. We were with him because he needed a band to play live, but honestly, he didn't need me to play keys in the studio. He played everything on the record.

He didn't sleep much. He just ate, slept, and drank music. He'd sit with a guitar or a keyboard and write. You can call it god or the universe of collective consciousness or whatever, but it meant there was music coming out of him. He could hear music in his head and it would flow through his fingers. He didn't write music. He'd record it in one take, instantly. It was like watching Mozart.

Just after he'd finished work on his second album, we were in this huge, beautiful studio in Denver, Colorado. Prince wanted to do something different.

The Rebels was a side project. Like a protégé band, but it was all of us. It featured every band member, writing their own material. Dez Dickerson, André Cymone, and Gayle Chapman all wrote stuff. It was done quickly, in about a week. Songs were being written in the studio, the day of recording. It was rocked out. Not much funk in there apart from André's instrumental.

Prince presented the idea to Warner Brothers. The second Prince album wasn't even out yet, so they thought a release under another name would confuse people. They didn't put it out. It was just overflow material."

OPPOSITE Performing his first concert to promote his debut album For You, *Capri Theater, Minneapolis, January 5, 1970.*

ABOVE *On stage at the Palace, Houston, Texas, December 1, 1979.*

RIGHT *Performing "Party Up" on Saturday Night Live, February 21, 1981.*

HIGH-HEEL BOOTS AND BIKINI BRIEFS

IN THE WORDS OF GAYLE CHAPMAN

"We had a tiff one day. I asked Prince why he and André would use the N-word with each other. He said it was none of my business. I got angry and asked why he'd hired me. 'Because you have blonde hair and blue eyes. You fit the bill.' I was hurt because I wondered what any of that had to do with my talent, but then he came back with 'You're the funkiest white chick I ever met.'

Our first big break was as the support act on the Rick James tour. Rick would get his crew together backstage with booze and joints and they would chant, 'Shit, Goddamn! Get off your ass and jam!' I said, 'We should have our own way of preparing.' I suggested a prayer and Prince was OK with it. We'd hold hands and I'd say 'Lord, thanks for keeping us focused. Let us go out and really stomp tonight in the name of Jesus Christ. Amen.' Pretty soon, Prince started leading the prayer. He was going on stage and singing about oral sex but he was acknowledging Jesus, too.

I think we were in Alabama and Prince had given us the set list. The way the whole thing was modeled was like putting a dick down the audience's throat. He wanted to say, 'OK, America! We're black, white, men and women, gender and race don't matter!' He was comfortable in high-heel boots and bikini briefs. He was embracing the idea that you can love in an unconventional way. It doesn't make you a bad person.

He put me out front doing dance moves in everyone's face. He would have me [facing up with my arms and legs on the ground in crab pose] on my back on all fours and pretend to play keyboard off my stomach. He'd stick his tongue down my throat. We were doing stuff on stage to suggest interracial promiscuity. It was intentional. He was hypersexual. The audience was all black kids. They loved him, but they would boo me."

*RIGHT Backstage pass for the Rick James'
Fire It Up tour, on which Prince was a
special guest, 1980.*

From left to right: At a photoshoot, date and location unknown; Bobby Z, Dez Dickerson, Lisa Coleman, Dr. Fink, Prince, and André Cymone.

ABOVE *From left to right: Bobby Z, Dr. Fink (on a leash),*
Brown Mark, Prince, Lisa Coleman, and Dez Dickerson.

WHEN YOU WERE MINE

IN THE WORDS OF DR. FINK

" In Orlando, we decided to have some fun being tourists. We wanted to go to Disneyland. We asked Prince to come along, too, but he said, 'Go ahead. Have fun.' I remember leaving him sitting outside his hotel room on the balcony, with his guitar. By the time we came back, he'd written 'When You Were Mine' for the third album.

The title track 'Dirty Mind' came from a rehearsal for a show. We were warming up and he liked a chord progression I was working on. I got to play the solo on 'Head,' so it was the start of Prince using the band a little more in the studio. It was incredibly DIY, though. The album was recorded in Prince's house. He even engineered it himself.

On *Controversy*, the band played on 'Jack U Off.' On *1999*, I pretty much played nothing. Dez Dickerson did some guitar on 'Little Red Corvette' and there were people doing vocals, but most of it was Prince. He could do it all himself. "

THE WAREHOUSE

IN THE WORDS OF HUCKY AUSTIN, SECURITY, 1982–1992

ABOVE LEFT Backstage pass for the Dirty Mind *tour, December 1980–April 1981.*

ABOVE RIGHT Backstage pass for the Controversy *tour, November 1981–March 1982.*

OPPOSITE On stage at the Bottom Line, New York City, February 15, 1980.

" My best friend was Brown Mark, Prince's bass player. I was a freshman in '82. I used to go to rehearsals in Prince's warehouse. They had just finished recording *1999* and they were getting ready to tour. I remember them doing 'Automatic,' 'Lady Cab Driver,' and also 'Wonderful Ass' that never came out. I would honestly go into some kind of trance watching the band. After months in that warehouse, Prince finally said my name as if I was his best buddy. They went off to tour and I decided I was gonna put some thighs on me and take a shot at becoming his bodyguard. "

"1999," "LITTLE RED CORVETTE," AND "DELIRIOUS" ARE PRINCE'S BIGGEST HITS TO DATE. HE MAKES IT ONTO MTV AND THE BEDROOM WALLS OF A MILLION AMERICAN TEENAGERS.

A WET NIGHT

IN THE WORDS OF DR. FINK

"By the time he was making *Purple Rain,* he wanted a real band vibe. We were now Prince and the Revolution. We'd been using the Minneapolis Dance Theatre as a rehearsal space, getting our dance moves ready for the movie, and he decided to do a benefit show for them at the club First Avenue. It was a hot, muggy Minneapolis night and the place was packed. It was wet. There was a lot of sweat in that room. I know it was August 3, 1983, because that's my mom's birthday. We didn't go out with the intention of getting a final take. We recorded it just in case. But that's where the song 'Purple Rain' comes from. Most of the album—'Let's Go Crazy', 'Computer Blue', 'I Would Die 4 U', and 'Baby I'm a Star'—was recorded on stage that night."

OPPOSITE Backstage during the 1999 tour, 1983.

PREVIOUS PAGE On stage during the Controversy tour, 1981.

DIZZYING

IN THE WORDS OF SUSAN ROGERS, SOUND ENGINEER, 1983–1987

" When I joined Prince in '83, he was preparing for the movie *Purple Rain*. He was about to make the movie. His star had already been rising for a long time. It was meteoric. When you're twenty-something and you're on top of the world and the work you are doing is being valued, why would you want to sleep?

Cognitively, he could be on output more than any human being I've ever seen. Typically, the brain needs to be on input as much or more time than it's on output. The extraordinary thing about Prince is the degree to how much he could make stuff. It's like a slingshot. He discovered he had a lot to say. He was catapulted with a very long trajectory of productivity.

It was dizzying. A song would become an album that would become a movie that would become another project. While he was on the road, he was also writing the next album. I had a big directory and I'd scout out studios along our touring route.

It felt like a tour of duty. I was joined at the hip to this person doing something wonderful. I was aware every single day how fortunate I was. This period in the '80s was just after New Wave and punk. A lot of it was driven by drum machines. A lot of it was technical in nature. It gave rise to new hairstyles, new clothes, and new lyrics. It was brand new and it belonged to us; those of us in our twenties. It mattered. We were making a new contribution that was different to the music that came before us. It matters to be doing music for your clan, your tribe. It was ours. Our generation's. "

HOODY

IN THE WORDS OF HUCKY AUSTIN

" Charles 'Big Chick' Huntsberry was heading Prince's security and he got me in. I got hired in as a bodyguard just before *Purple Rain*. It was my first tour.

The jump from *Controversy* to *1999* had been big, but *Purple Rain* was another planet. The album had just come out and I think the movie was about to drop. You remember he was wearing these sparkly hoodies? Well, we went to see the Jacksons' Victory tour and Prince wore this thing to keep covered up.

We're in this stadium in Texas with 80,000 people and we walk to the soundboard. Big Chick, who was heading security, told us, 'Whatever you do, don't run.' It was all fine. Prince was covered, we were watching the show. You know what Prince did? He took his hood off. Next thing someone screams, 'It's Prince!' and we have half the stadium chasing us. Prince and Michael were the biggest stars on the planet. It was just hysteria, like when the Beatles come to town. He was more nimble than the rest of us. He was out the door! Outside, Chick got real mad with Prince. Real upset. Prince said, 'Sorry. I won't do that no more.' God knows why he took his hood off. "

THE BEAUTIFUL ONES ON A PURPLE CARPET

IN THE WORDS OF HUCKY AUSTIN

" I was in L.A. because *Purple Rain* was scheduled to premiere. The city was abuzz with excitement. Beautiful cars, beautiful people, money, money, money.

Prince's entourage stayed at the Westwood Marquis. The hotel was filled with celebrities who had arrived to attend the premiere. Before the screening, I recall stepping out of my room into the hallway and seeing Peabo Bryson. Now, of course, I did a double take, because I hadn't expected to see him. He apparently feared I was a crazy fan or would be asking for his autograph or something, and promptly dropped his eyes and actually tried to cover his face! It struck me as funny, so I told Prince. Well, wouldn't you know it, later that day I was in the elevator with Prince on the way back to his room and Mr. Bryson steps into the elevator. He looked at me and realized I was with Prince, who promptly averted his eyes and tried to cover his face. After we exited the elevator, Prince gave me his devilish little smirk.

Mann's Chinese Theatre was hosting the premiere and, in preparation, had decked the place out with purple accents, including a purple carpet. I remember Pee-wee Herman rode up in a go-kart. Stevie Nicks, Eddie Murphy, Little Richard, John Cougar, Lionel Richie, and a host of other celebrities walked the purple carpet, eagerly anticipating the screening. Warner Brothers had a custom purple limousine deliver Prince to the theater. When he got out, looking his glam-rock-funk best, the crowd went absolutely crazy. "

BELOW LEFT Access All Areas pass for the Purple Rain *tour, November 1984–April 1985.*

BELOW RIGHT Guest pass for the Purple Rain *tour, June 17, 1985.*

OPPOSITE On stage, celebrating his birthday at the First Avenue Club in Minneapolis, June 7, 1984.

ABOVE The premiere of Purple Rain at Mann's Chinese Theatre, Hollywood, California, July 26, 1984.

HE HAS A NUMBER 1 SINGLE, ALBUM, AND MOVIE AT THE SAME TIME. *PURPLE RAIN* SELLS MORE THAN TWENTY MILLION COPIES. CRITICAL ACCLAIM, PUBLIC ADORATION, GRAMMIES, AND AN OSCAR ALL BELONG TO PRINCE.

START LEARNING THIS

IN THE WORDS OF DR. FINK

" He told us that the tour would end and he would go on hiatus. We'd only done the USA, I wanted to go to Europe, Australia, and Japan but he wasn't interested.

It took about three-and-a-half months for him to have the next album done. That record, *Around the World in a Day,* is accredited to Prince and the Revolution, but it's mainly Prince with Wendy and Lisa. Bobby, Brown Mark, and me weren't really involved. One day he handed me a cassette and said, 'OK, start learning this.'

'What happened with your hiatus?'

'I'm done with the hiatus.' "

ABOVE On stage at the Forum, Inglewood, California, February 19, 1985.

HIS SHOW

IN THE WORDS OF SAINT PAUL PETERSON, PROTÉGÉ, 1984–1985

"The Time had broken up. I'd been playing keys in that band. I was sitting in our rehearsal space warehouse. Prince sat us in a circle. He looked at me and said, 'Everyone has gone but I'm going to have a new band and you're gonna be the lead singer.' I was nineteen and it scared the hell out of me.

He'd send cassette tapes to my mom's house. I was that young. The songs were complete and had Prince on vocals. I'd learn the tape and go in to record the vocal as closely as I could. It was David Z's job to make sure I executed what those vocals were. There was a specific sound Prince was looking for. It was his show."

ABOVE *On stage celebrating his birthday at the First Avenue Club in Minneapolis, June 7, 1984.*

LIKE CASTING A MOVIE

IN THE WORDS OF ALAN LEEDS, TOUR MANAGER, 1983–1989; PRESIDENT OF PAISLEY PARK RECORDS, 1989–1993

"He was like a funnel. It was like someone was pouring songs into him and they just continued to spill out of him. Instead of water it was songs. Being as prolific as he was, it was almost inevitable that he would create alter egos. If Prince was a girl, he'd have been Vanity 6. If he was a pure funk musician, he would have been the Time. If he was a jazz musician, he would have been Madhouse. I'm surprised he didn't come up with a country music concept—cowboy Prince! He was having a field day.

He would record template vocals for the satellite projects as a road map. The most extreme example was *The Family* album. Prince recorded all of those songs himself and then replaced his vocal with Paul's and Susannah's. He paid enormous detail to the phrasing and modulations in the voice. He had Paul all but photocopy his vocals. The same with Vanity 6 and Apollonia 6 projects. Conversely, Sheila E. had much more leeway. Jill Jones had a lot of freedom, and to this day I think her album is one of the better Paisley Park records. Morris Day and the Time had a fair amount of influence, too. It varied from project to project.

It was as if these projects were stage plays that Prince had written and produced, so he cast them the same way you would cast a movie. The problem is, when Morris became a star, he was playing a role that Prince created. Everything down to the comb and the mirror on stage is Prince. The Family and Madhouse—in fact, almost all of the satellite projects—were entirely Prince creations. These groups featured incredibly talented people, but the artists themselves begin to feel pigeonholed. That's what happened with Jam and Lewis in the Time. There was no place for them to apply their craft. There was only room for one master."

OPPOSITE On stage during the Purple Rain *tour, 1985.*

LAB RAT

" I'm not a fan of Prince's music. And I've never been. I became involved with the Family because my brother Alan was his tour manager. He told me he was putting a new group together and he wanted a saxophone player. Alan played him a tape of me and he was suitably impressed.

I had no aspiration to be involved with him or an artist like that. His persona did not interest me. My brother said, 'Besides all that, this guy is a remarkable musician and you will find that worthwhile.' He was absolutely right.

There were an awful lot of times that Prince would call me into the studio and he would not be there. Prince might call me and say, 'Just do whatever you want with this,' or he might give me specifics, 'I need a solo. I need a lead line.' Whatever.

That was kind of telling me that it was a song that was not going to see the light of day. He just had to record music because that's all he knows how to do. If he wasn't there, nine times out of ten, it would tell me it was nothing of any particular importance to him.

If Prince was in studio, then it was interesting for me, especially because he was still figuring things out. He'd direct me and give me parameters. I'd think, 'OK, I'll be your lab rat.' The times he wanted me to throw my experience aside, that's when it was fun. He could use me as a color in his palette. I was fortunate because he didn't play the saxophone. He'd get me to play a character in the 'movie' of the song. He was the screenwriter, the actor, and the producer. That's how he looked at all of his projects. That's how he looks at his career. His whole life is a movie. He invented himself. "

OPPOSITE *On stage during the* Purple Rain *tour at the Summit, Houston, Texas, January 10, 1985.*

PARADE AND AN ANONYMOUS PURPLE LIMOUSINE

IN THE WORDS OF BRENT FISCHER, ORCHESTRAL ARRANGER IN COLLABORATION WITH CLARE FISCHER 1985–2009

"It was 1985. I was twenty-one and still hanging out at my father's house almost every day. Prince was in Minneapolis and we were in L.A. We were sent a cassette tape labeled 'Marx Brothers Project,' which turned out to be the *Parade* album without the orchestration. My father would decide what instrumentation to use and then work out the arrangements. We wrote to surround the vocal or instruments with lush orchestration.

In the first session, we planned to record two songs. We were told Prince would join us, but for whatever reason, on the day, he couldn't make it. When he heard the results, he called my father and said, 'If I'd have been there, things may have turned out differently.' It wasn't a bad thing. Not at all. He was really impressed, so he told my father he would never show up to a session again. He stuck to his word for the rest of their working relationship. My father and Prince worked together on dozens of songs and never met once.

There were a few close calls. Prince wanted incidental music for the movie *Under the Cherry Moon*. It wasn't part of the *Parade* album, so my father asked him to send a videotape of the scene to help the writing. Prince agreed, so a day later there was a knock at the door. I opened it and saw a purple limousine outside the house. The limo driver was on the doorstep and he had a videotape. I said, 'I can take that.' But I was told there were very specific instructions for the tape to be delivered 'directly to the hands of Clare Fischer.' I called up to my father, who came down and picked up the tape. As soon as the door shut my father said, 'I don't know how to work the VCR!' We watched the scene together and talked about what we would do for the music. I think Prince was probably in the purple limo, but we never really knew for certain."

OPPOSITE   Ready to release the motion picture Under the Cherry Moon, *1986.*

KISS

IN THE WORDS OF ERIC LEEDS

"Right before the *Parade* album came out, he still hadn't decided what the album was going to be. He was sitting with Wendy and I in the studio. He was in a playful mood. He said, 'Considering these songs and anything else we've done recently, sequence me an album. I'm curious to see what you'd do.' The first thing I took off the album was 'Kiss.' I thought it was a nothing song. I didn't care for it then and I still don't to this day. He didn't listen to me. It shows what I know about pop music!"

THE FLESH

IN THE WORDS OF ERIC LEEDS

"There was a week when I was out in L.A. at Sunset Sound. Sheila, Wendy, Lisa, Prince, and I would go into the studio and just play. That was some of the most enjoyable stuff for me.

There was one extemporaneous jam we did. Jonathan Melvoin and Levi Seacer were on it, too. It went on for forty-five minutes. It was recorded to two-track and some of it was absolutely fabulous. Prince threw all that stuff to me and said, 'Edit it. Do what you want with it. Make me an album.' I cut it down to twenty-five minutes for one side of the record and sequenced an album. For two or three days it was the greatest thing in the world to him.

He thought about releasing that as an instrumental project called *The Flesh*. Some of it, little bits and pieces, ended up as incidental music for the movie *Under the Cherry Moon*. It was cool, but it was really just us jerking off."

OPPOSITE   *On stage during the* Parade *tour,*
Wembley Arena, London, August 1986.

THE LEAKING THUNDERBIRD
IN THE WORDS OF SUSAN ROGERS

" Prince's employee was also his half brother Duane. He was Prince's valet, among other things. He would make sure his car, the Thunderbird, was taken to the car wash. Prince did what a lot of us did at the time. If we had a song, we would print it onto a cassette. Prince would drive around in the car playing it. When he was done, he would toss it onto the back seat. A lot of things were finding their way onto the black market. It turned out it was the car wash. The people who were detailing the car had access to the back seat; a treasure trove of unreleased music. "

YOU ONLY MAKE LOVE FOR THE FIRST TIME, ONCE
IN THE WORDS OF ALAN LEEDS

" There was a period from late '85 when Prince was in a casually collaborative mood. Sheila E., my brother Eric, Wendy, and Lisa were sharing a lot of old music. They made it a mission to turn him on to new things. I don't think Prince was steeped in jazz at that point.

I remember my brother saying, 'I just played *Duke Ellington Live at Newport* for Prince and he flipped out!' They were as excited about sharing stuff with him as he was about sharing stuff with them. I don't think my brother knew much about Joni Mitchell. They were kind of growing together as musicians.

There was a season of sessions in Prince's home and Sunset Sound in L.A., where he was recording songs cowritten by Wendy, Lisa, and sometimes Sheila. Songs like 'In a Large Room with No Light' and 'Power Fantastic.' Some of us that had access to the demos listened to them religiously, as fans.

It may be the most creative period in his whole career. He was an established artist with the experienced skills of an adult, but he had the passion of someone that hadn't done everything. He was still hungry for new sounds and ideas. Of course, he has made brilliant music since, but you're only new at something once. You only make love for the first time, once. "

ABOVE On stage during the Parade *tour, Rotterdam,*
August 1986.

CAN I PLAY WITH U?

IN THE WORDS OF ERIC LEEDS

"Prince and I did a song, ostensibly for Miles Davis, called 'Can I Play with U?' They were considering it for Miles's first Warner Brothers recording *Tutu*. There were people in Miles's camp who were very interested in it, for the cachet of having a Prince song.

Miles dubbed trumpet on it. I said, 'Oh boy, it gets me into the Miles Davis discography!'

Prince asked me about it, but I think it was a fait accompli and he had already decided that he didn't want to release the song. As much as it might have had the cool factor of being on a Miles Davis record, it was just not that good and it was never released."

LEFT On stage during the Parade *tour,*
with Eric Leeds, 1986.

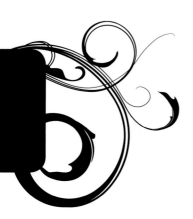

THE TALE OF THE FINEST FELINE

IN THE WORDS OF CAT GLOVER, DANCER/VOCALS, 1987–1988

" I made it onto the show *Star Search,* all the way to the finals. Everyone was watching that show. I became friends with Devin DeVasquez, a model who'd been hanging with Prince. One day she asked if I wanted to go to dinner at his place in Beverly Hills.

We were sitting at this huge sixteen-seat dining table, just hanging out. Prince's dad was there and Steve Fargnoli, who was part of Prince's management at the time. Eventually, Prince came in and checked everyone out. He knew every person around the table except me, so when our eyes met there was some curiosity on his face. He told Steve, 'Come upstairs and listen to something.' They both left the room and a minute later I heard what become known as 'Housequake' coming through the ceiling. The bass was heavy. It sounded hot.

We finished up dinner and headed out to a private club. We were sitting in a booth and Prince said, 'Will you dance with me?' I think it was some Robert Palmer. We got up and started moving. I was taller than him, but I didn't want to duck. I tried to relax and enjoy it. I was wearing leather gloves, hand in hand with Prince, and I remember thinking, 'Oh shit. I can't feel his actual skin!' We grooved. I'd copy him and he'd copy me. He was checking to see if I could keep up.

Prince sat down with Steve and started talking. This place was bourgie. The kind of setup where everyone sits around looking cool. Tony Curtis and a bunch of Hollywood stars were there, but that didn't scare me. I turned it out. I asked the DJ to play house music. I'm from Chicago, you know? I was dancing on the DJ box, on tables, and on anything I could stand on. I was fearless.

When I sat down, Steve whispered into my ear, 'Prince really likes you. He wants to put you in his new girl group.' At that point, no one knew I could sing or rap or anything. The girl group didn't happen, but a few weeks later I joined Prince's band. He told me I'd need to wear flat shoes because he didn't want me to look taller than him. As he put it: 'When we're dancing, I'll look like I'm taking my horse for a walk.' "

OPPOSITE On stage during the Parade *tour, 1986.*

IN THE WORDS OF SUSAN ROGERS

" I can tell you what I remember. I've thought about this a lot. It was winter in Minneapolis, a few months after Prince had broken off his engagement with Susannah Melvoin, the twin sister of Wendy. He called me in to record that day at his home studio. It was just the two of us. I think it was on the weekend. He left me a note saying what he wanted; sounds that were big, long reverb. It was going to be a ballad.

It starts with spoken word. He was speaking to Wally. Wally was a member of his crew at that time; one of the dancers on stage. He's talking about wanting to go out and he compliments Wally on his glasses. 'Can I try them on? I'm going to a party tonight and I want to look good,' he's saying, 'I want to go out because I just broke up with someone and I want to see if I can get someone new.'

There's a melody underneath. He goes into a chorus repeating, 'Oh my la de da. Oh my la de da.' It's a play on words because it's like 'oh my melody' and also, 'oh my malady'—my sickness. It breaks down. There's a crescendo. The song gets huge. He layers the backing vocals and the piano gets really big. It breaks down. He says to Wally: 'You can have your glasses back. I'm not going out.'

It was beautiful. Just beautiful. The arrangements, the idea, the expressions; just gorgeous. After we finished recording, he said, 'Put all twenty-four tracks in record and erase it.' He said it very calmly. I said 'No. Think about it. Sleep on it.' He said, 'I'll do it.' He put all twenty-four tracks in record, ready. He hit record and erased it. It was gone.

I was naive. I didn't know about artistic nature. It taught me why artists create. They create to say something. Just because you've said something, it doesn't mean you want it heard. It's like a diary. Sometimes you just want to get it out. He didn't want it heard. He didn't want it known. "

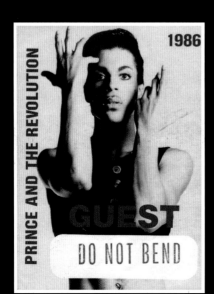

PRINCE AND THE REVOLUTION

1986

GUEST

DO NOT BEND

LEFT Guest pass for the Parade *tour, 1986.*

OPPOSITE Prince's Paisley Park Studio, Chanhassen, *Minnesota, shortly after completion.*

MADHOUSE

IN THE WORDS OF ERIC LEEDS

" We did a couple of projects called Madhouse. The first album was released anonymously. We did the whole thing in three days, beginning to end. It was a person who is not a jazz musician wanting to be a jazz musician. One of the reasons he didn't want his name associated with it is he didn't want the jazz community criticizing it.

The marketing thing of Madhouse became an in-joke between us. We put together a backstory that was just completely fictional. There was no one credited on the first album at all. Not even me. For the press and marketing campaign, we sat and came up with fictitious names for the musicians. They were fellas that I had supposedly known when I was living in Atlanta. That worked really well until I was interviewed by a music writer from Atlanta. He said, 'I've lived in Atlanta all my life and I know the music scene inside out, but I don't know any of these guys.' "

THE VAULT

IN THE WORDS OF SUSAN ROGERS

I put as many of the multitrack tapes as I could in one place, but I realized there were many pieces missing. I asked people who worked with him, 'Where can I find the masters for this or for that?' They said, 'They are probably at Warner Brothers or Burbank in California or Sunset Sound.' I got on the phone and called around, 'Do you have any Prince tapes there? Could you send them to me?'

It became an obsession. My goal was to have everything he's ever recorded right here. I started amassing tapes. That's when the office gave me a computer. I made a database. Then we began planning Paisley Park and we thought, 'If we're gonna have a vault, let's have a vault.' Because if we get a tornado or a flood, this is his legacy. We need to preserve these things.

It is a bank vault. It's really thick and it has a wheel on it. It's also a storm shelter. When I left in '87 it was nearly full. I can't imagine what was done after that.

Prince taught me that every album would have a kernel or seed. Maybe in his case, six to seven songs that constitute the heart of the record. These are the statements that came closest to saying what he wanted to say at that time. Other songs were chosen to support the heart of the record. Songs like 'I Could Never Take the Place of Your Man' or 'Slow Love' are examples. They were recorded and put in the vault until such time at which they would become useful. When we sequence a record and think 'we need something up-tempo here' or 'something that is not lyrically deep,' we could get something out of the vault.

What took a lot of time was deciding what songs would come together to make an album. There was a song called 'Moonbeam Levels.' Just so beautiful. Occasionally, when we were sequencing records, we'd put it in the sequence. But he'd always pull it. It never made it onto an album. He just didn't want to say it.

OPPOSITE On stage during the Sign O' the Times *tour, 1987.*

THE BLACK ALBUM
IN THE WORDS OF SUSAN ROGERS

"We had been working at Sunset Sound in L.A. for a long time on *Sign O' the Times*. We needed to take a break. To stop for a minute. To do something different. Prince wanted to record something to dance to at Sheila E.'s birthday party. Back in those days, you could record something in the studio, take it to Grunberg Mastering on Sunset Boulevard, and have it mastered and pressed into an acetate. You can take that to a club and play it on the turntable. So that's what we did.

We recorded 'Rock Hard in a Funky Place,' '2 Nigs United 4 West Compton,' a lot of those tracks, just to dance to at the party. It was rapid. It was fun. I believe his intention was not to put them out. It was after *Sign O' the Times* came out that we sequenced them and it became an album."

THE TALE OF THE FINEST FELINE II

IN THE WORDS OF CAT GLOVER

"I wanted to work hard and do well. I learned every lyric on the song 'Crystal Ball,' even the parts I wasn't meant to sing. We never got to perform it live because it didn't come out. The record company wouldn't let him put out a triple album. It became *Sign O' the Times* and we headed out on tour.

I was the youngest in the band and incredibly naive. I'd never experienced attention like that. It's like being in a movie. He would tell me not to be afraid and call me his 'finest feline.' I remember being in Europe and teasing, 'Prince, why are you so boring? Why is everything you do about celebrity?' We were on the tour bus and Prince took us to McDonalds and ordered cheeseburgers for everyone. It was his way of saying, 'I can be normal, too.'

Prince liked the fact that I was a street dancer. He liked how regular I was. I took him away from those bourgeois places to the underground clubs. I knew those places inside out. You could say I ran them so no one would bother Prince. He was always a club kid. On *The Black Album* in 'Cindy C' I say, 'Serve it up, Frankie!' I'm talking about Frankie Knuckles. I introduced Prince to Chicago house. It gave him a new energy. He loved going to watch people dance. He loved looking at people's hairstyles and outfits. Why do you think he would do so many aftershows at clubs? It was his way of staying connected."

LEFT V.I.P. pass for the Sign O' the Times *tour, May–June 1987.*

OPPOSITE Cat Glover and Eric Leeds on stage during the Sign O' the Times tour, Isstadion, Stockholm, Sweden, May 9, 1987.

NINE MONTHS AFTER *SIGN O' THE TIMES,* PRINCE IS SET TO FOLLOW UP WITH *THE BLACK ALBUM.* THE RECORD IS SHIPPED, BUT DAYS BEFORE ITS RELEASE, HE CHANGES HIS MIND, MAKING IT THE MOST WIDELY BOOTLEGGED ALBUM OF ALL TIME.

LOVESEXY

IN THE WORDS OF ALAN LEEDS

"One of my fondest memories of Prince in studio was during the making of *Lovesexy.* On a regular day, he'd come into the office at Paisley Park in the morning. He'd look at his mail and have a brief meeting if there was business to deal with. Then he'd disappear into the studio with some lyrics he'd written the night before. By five or six, I'd get a call and he'd say, 'You wanna hear something?'

He would play the music unbearably loud. Conversation was impossible and so was ignoring the music, because you felt it in every bone of your body. I remember on one occasion, we were listening to 'Anna Stesia' or perhaps 'Alphabet St.' and he began shouting in my ear. He was describing the video concept while playing the song he'd just recorded. At the end of the playback, I looked at him and said, 'You mean to tell me; not only have you made this song today, you already have a video concept in your head?' The pace was quite remarkable."

OPPOSITE *On stage during the Sign O' the Times tour, Palais Omnisports de Paris, Bercy, Paris, June 15, 1987.*

THE BADDEST BAND IN THE WORLD

IN THE WORDS OF STEVE PARKE,
ART DIRECTOR, 1988–2001

"I met Levi Seacer Jr. backstage at a Sheila E. show. She was supporting Lionel Richie and Levi played guitar in the band. I told Levi I was an artist and I drew a picture of him on a napkin. We stayed in touch. One day he called and said, 'Guess who's gonna be in Prince's new band?' He showed Prince a bunch of my work and eventually I got a call.

My first real job with Prince was painting the set for the 'Glam Slam' video. Prince had already parted ways with my predecessor. I knew that if I was going to stay, I had to do something mind-blowing. Prince was in Paris. I was twenty-five, a young man, so I stayed up for three days straight to get one-third of the set finished. I looked around Paisley Park and tried to incorporate things that I saw, like his clothes. When Prince was back I didn't hear anything. I asked Levi, 'What do you think will happen?' Levi said: 'Well, did Prince say anything to you? No? Well, that means he likes it!'

That turned into me doing the *Lovesexy* tour stage. I remember the band being a little upset, because the original album artwork featured the whole band. When they found out the cover was actually going to be a naked Prince with flowers and stamens all over the place, they were kind of bummed. It was shot by Jean-Baptiste Mondino and completely beautiful, but my twenty-something guy brain thought, 'People might not buy that.'

It didn't matter how tired I was, or how long I'd been painting, every day I'd come in to watch the rehearsals. Prince was on an emotional and spiritual high that he wanted to share that with everyone. It wasn't all poetry though. He worked that band for eight hours a day. I remember one time things just weren't working. He said, 'Clearly you guys don't want to work today, so go home.' He just walked away.

A little later, I was painting and I overheard Prince bragging to some of the management team: 'I have the baddest band in the world. No one can beat them!' An hour earlier he kicks them out and now he's saying about how great they are? He could kick your ass and even embarrass you, but it was just his way of always lifting the bar higher."

BELOW *Prince and the band sound check, Feijenoord Stadion, Rotterdam, August 17, 1988. From left to right: Levi Seacer Jr., Cat Glover, Prince, and Miko Weaver.*

GWEN RECORDS

IN THE WORDS OF ALAN LEEDS

Lovesexy wasn't received as well as he hoped. I remember sitting in Paisley Park with *Billboard* magazine and Prince pointing out the records charting higher than him were by nonmusicians. He understood the industry machine and how it could benefit him. He used it masterfully on occasion, the *Batman* soundtrack being an example. He got another number one album and single out of *Batman*. But if things didn't turn out the way he wanted, he decided that the fault was with management and the record company, ignoring decisions that he had himself made. It wasn't really Warner Brothers that he was frustrated with. It was the industry model.

By 1990, he was exploring alternative ways of getting his music out. He suggested we release records to the public through an infomercial. He told me, 'We should go for a ten-minute commercial on late-night TV and send the records through the mail!' He was serious. It was like the music version of a George Foreman grill. I reminded him of the fact we were in a joint venture record deal with Warner Brothers Records. He said, 'OK, we'll put the label in your name and use a pseudonym for me.' I explained that Warner were paying half my salary and I had legal obligations. 'Well put it in your wife's name, then. It will be Gwen Records. Let's just get the stuff out.'

OPPOSITE *On stage during the* Nude *tour, 1990.*

A NUDE TORNADO

IN THE WORDS OF STEVE PARKE

"Early on, I'd realized that Prince had a hand in everything. There was one moment I was looking at him standing in a hallway that kind of explained him to me. It was around the time of the *Nude* tour. He was prepping the *Graffiti Bridge* movie and album and getting ready for the shows. He was coming out of a rehearsal. To the right of him there was video editing going on. Left was the studio and upstairs was wardrobe. I looked at him and thought, 'He is in the eye of a tornado.' He loved that. He reveled in things happening. It meant things were moving forward and there was no stagnation. Everything was an extension of his creativity. That's pretty fucking spectacular. He needed to be engaged in it all."

ABOVE On stage with Miko Weaver during the Nude *tour, National Exhibition Centre, Birmingham, June 29, 1990.*

OPPOSITE On stage during the Nude *tour, Wembley Arena, London, July 1990.*

TACTILE MEMORIES OF THE NEW POWER GENERATION

IN THE WORDS OF MICHAEL BLAND, DRUMS, INTERMITTENTLY 1990–2015

I was playing in Dr. Mambo's Combo at Bunkers, in downtown Minneapolis. Prince would come and sit in every couple of weeks. My friends would say, 'Dude, you're gonna play with Prince!' I was a kid when he offered me the job and he was quite forgiving. Before the first tour, during rehearsal, I stopped Prince when he was leaving to ask, 'What time is my flight tomorrow?' He probably thought, 'How the hell do I know, I'm too busy writing hits!' But he was polite and told me who to check with.

A lot of the crew who'd been around for a while told me Prince would jump in a lot with the drummers who came before me. He would show them exactly how he wanted them to play. He didn't do that with me. It gave me a lot of confidence.

We'd record whenever he felt like recording. During the *Nude* tour in 1990, we had a long run in London. Prince wanted to do sixteen shows at Wembley Arena, because Dire Straits had just sold out eleven. The promoter said, 'Prince, you're crazy.' Prince said, 'Book the shows.' And you know what? They all sold out.

Every night we'd go back to shower at the hotel and then head out. It was either the club Stringfellows or Olympic Studios. Being out with Prince isn't too much fun, because you're boxed in by security and there's a hungry public trying to get a look. I preferred hitting the studio and working. We worked on Rosie Gaines's record at the time. We laid down 'Daddy Pop' for the *Diamonds and Pearls* album, too.

I have a tactile memory, so I really feel a lot when I hear specific songs now. We recorded 'Willing and Able,' 'Strollin',' and 'Money Don't Matter 2 Night' in the same night in Tokyo. We were in this small studio. I had stomach flu, but I just had to muscle through it. I didn't feel great and I wasn't playing great. To this day, when I hear those songs, I feel a little nauseous.

OPPOSITE On stage during the Nude *tour, Wembley Arena, London, July 1990.*

FAR RIGHT All access pass for the Nude *tour, June–September 1990.*

RIGHT Pass for the Diamond and Pearls *tour, April–July 1992.*

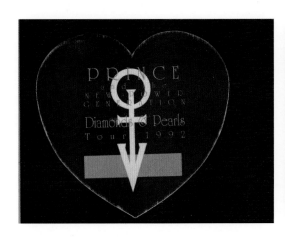

MARTIKA'S KITCHEN

IN THE WORDS OF MARTIKA, SINGER/SONGWRITER

"I was preparing for my second album. 'Toy Soldiers' had been a hit, so the record company was backing me. One of the execs said, 'Who do you want to work with?' Naturally, I said, 'Prince.'

Less than a week passed and I was on a plane to Minneapolis. I'd grown up singing, 'Paisley Park is in your heart.' Now as a twenty year old with butterflies in my stomach, I was on my way there! I was taken to the sound stage. The whole band was there. It was like going to a concert hall and being the only person in the audience. He walked over with that long, feathered *Graffiti Bridge* hair and said, 'If you don't mind, we're going to do a few songs.' I was mesmerized.

Afterward, we sat in his office. Right away, he said, 'This is a gift for you. I wrote it last night.' He handed me the lyrics to 'Martika's Kitchen.' I sat there reading 'Come and get some in Martika's kitchen, baby. You bring the noise and I'll bring the smile.' I thought, 'He wrote me a theme song!'

He looked at some poems I'd written. He said he'd be in touch, so I went back to L.A. A week later, a cassette arrived with Prince singing 'Martika's Kitchen,' 'Love. . . Thy Will Be Done,' 'Spirit,' 'Don't Say You Love Me,' and 'Open Book.' He'd incorporated a lot of the poems I'd written in my book. I had friends over and they ran around the living room screaming, 'He's singing your name, dude!' "

RIGHT   *Image from the motion picture* Graffiti Bridge, *released on November 2, 1990.*

HARRIET TUBMAN INSPIRES THE "GETT OFF" VIDEO

IN THE WORDS OF HUCKY AUSTIN

" I would wear a bandana. It was my thing. I'd wear it backward, with the knot at the front. I've always done it. Prince was a prankster. He liked to laugh, so one day I'm wearing my bandana and in front of everyone he shouts, 'You look like Harriet Tubman!'

Two days later, he's getting ready to shoot the video for 'Gett Off' and I show up for work. Prince is wearing a bandana on his head with the knot at the front! I said, 'I thought I looked like Harriet?' He laughed: 'You do, but I wear it sexy.' "

DIAMONDS AND PEARLS IS PRINCE'S BIGGEST-SELLING RECORD SINCE PURPLE RAIN. HE SIGNS A NEW SIX-ALBUM DEAL WORTH A REPORTED $100,000,000, MAKING PRINCE THE HIGHEST-PAID RECORDING STAR IN THE INDUSTRY.

AN UNCONSCIOUS PLANE

IN THE WORDS OF MICHAEL BLAND

" There are moments of invincibility. Something about that particular time meant anything I wanted to play was right at my fingertips. Coming off tour, the band was kinetically connected, so a lot of those tracks on the *Love Symbol* album just came. 'The Morning Papers' was done in one take. 'And God Created Woman' was another one. I did all of that ornate drumming, almost unconsciously, on my first pass. Prince was like 'Thank you, sir!' Not only is he imbued with this spirit, it gets into you as well. You are sharing a space. You get into an unconscious plane. That is what I remember most about that time. "

OPPOSITE In silhouette, on stage during the Diamonds and Pearls *tour, Ahoy, Rotterdam, May 27, 1992.*

LIKE A FREIGHT TRAIN

IN THE WORDS OF SONNY THOMPSON

"We were all tight. We were all friends. We all really liked being around each other. Sometimes he would come in with structure, but often we'd rehearse and then he'd want to start writing something. The more you play, the more things come out. There was chemistry. 'Sexy MF' was made like that. We were playing around with some ideas and all of a sudden that bass came to me. I thought, 'This needs to sound like a freight train' and boom, it just locked."

OPPOSITE   With the New Power Generation. From left to right: Sonny T., Morris Hayes, Prince, Levi Seacer Jr., Mayte (masked), and the Hornheads.

THE UNDERTAKER

IN THE WORDS OF FAFU, DRUM PROGRAMMING, 1994–1996

" I was friends with Prince's drummer, Michael Bland. That meant I got to go to shows at Paisley Park as Michael's guest. It was summer '93 and the band was getting ready to head out to Europe. In the rehearsal space, there were two setups. On one side, the full band thing with keys and horns. On the other side, a stripped-down set for what we were calling the Power Trio. It was just Prince on vocals and guitar, Michael on drums, and Sonny on bass. Prince would rehearse the full setup in the day and the stripped down band at night.

Michael doesn't drive, so there was perhaps a two-week period where he asked me to be his driver. He was always getting called into Paisley at crazy hours, so he needed someone to be on call to give him a ride. One night, he called me and said he needed to get to work. We got to the studio after one a.m. Prince's guitar tech looked at me and said, 'OK, sit in the corner.' There was just the band, two technicians, and a two-man camera crew in the room. You know, one of those old shoulder-mounted cameras with a cord coming out of the back? That was it.

Prince said: 'I'm about to record an album. Make sure the sound is right.' They ran right through seven tracks. From 'The Ride' to 'Dolphin.' It was recording straight to DAT exactly as you hear on the finished thing. No overdubs. Nothing. It was a different way of doing things for Prince at the time. He had a forty-eight-track console and I knew he would often fill up everything. You could say some of that stuff from that period was overproduced. But this was the opposite of that.

I think it was his way of showing everyone he was an amazing guitarist. Not just the sex symbol, androgynous pop star with crazy hair we knew. It was called *The Undertaker* and it was meant to come out as a cover mount with a magazine. The record company wouldn't allow it. The footage turned into a film that's cut with a model walking around, crying, and throwing up.

I watched him record an entire album in one take. I dropped Michael off at his house at about four. It seemed pretty normal back then. "

OPPOSITE *Performing on stage during the Act II tour, Brabanthallen, Den Bosch, The Netherlands, August 9, 1993.*

❝ *I THINK IT WAS HIS WAY OF SHOWING EVERYONE
HE WAS AN AMAZING GUITARIST. NOT JUST THE SEX
SYMBOL, ANDROGYNOUS POP STAR WITH CRAZY HAIR
WE KNEW.* **❞**

FAFU

APRIL 27, 1993. PRINCE ANNOUNCES HIS RETIREMENT FROM STUDIO RECORDING TO EXPLORE "LIVE THEATER, NIGHTCLUBS, AND MOTION PICTURES."

WEEKS LATER, ON HIS THIRTY-FIFTH BIRTHDAY, PRINCE DECLARES HE HAS BECOME ♀.

FOURTEEN ALBUMS IN, WARNER BROTHERS RECORDS PREPARE TO RELEASE THE FIRST-EVER PRINCE'S HITS PACKAGE.

PRESERVATION
IN THE WORDS OF MICHAEL BLAND

"There was quite a rush to save a lot of the tapes in the vault around the time *The Hits/The B-Sides* package came out. The company wanted various gems and whatnot. Prince realized some of those tapes sitting in the vault had attrition. They were dissolving.

There's a process called baking, which means the tapes are slowly warmed up, so they can be played. They had to cook the tapes in a kiln, because they had decomposed. The only way to save them was to cook 'em.

There was a mad dash to do a lot of that at that time. 'Power Fantastic' and '4 the Tears in Your Eyes' ended up on that package. Then sometime in '93 going into '94, the digital machine turned up and that took things to the next stage. That stuff is safe. I think."

SURE, WHO'S CALLING?
IN THE WORDS OF MICHAEL VAN HUFFEL, ART ASSISTANT/ART DIRECTOR, 1994–2000

"This must have been '94 or '95 or something, because I'd just started working for him. The phone rings, my wife Lisa picks up, and a deep voice asks, 'Is Michael there?' Lisa says, 'Sure. Who's calling?' That was the end of the call.

Five minutes later, his assistant would call and say, 'The boss wants to talk to Michael.' He was taking the name change really, really seriously. If you asked who was calling, he would hang up the phone. That happened a few times until we worked out it was better not to ask."

OPPOSITE On stage during the Act II tour, 1993.

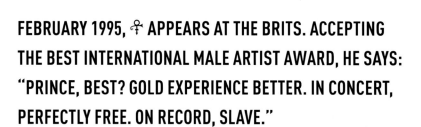

FEBRUARY 1995, ♀ APPEARS AT THE BRITS. ACCEPTING THE BEST INTERNATIONAL MALE ARTIST AWARD, HE SAYS: "PRINCE, BEST? GOLD EXPERIENCE BETTER. IN CONCERT, PERFECTLY FREE. ON RECORD, SLAVE."

A PRODUCT OF HIS OWN IMAGINATION

IN THE WORDS OF MICHAEL BLAND

" Prince had given an interview in a magazine where he mentioned *The Gold Experience*. That's where Mo Ostin, the executive at Warner Brothers, heard about it. The genesis of the dispute, in my opinion, was a conversation Prince had with Ostin. He said something like, 'When you get that finished, send it over and we'll do what we do.' That led to a discussion about intellectual property [in which] . . . Prince was really offended . . . .

His way of creating music didn't match the industry. A lot of artists think, 'OK, great, time to create a record.' They book studio time. It's a thing they have to go through. They have A&R on the phone offering advice because they're concerned about their end of the money. They'll say, 'You can't go out at this time, because Taylor Swift has a record out and your audience is similar to her audience.' Prince exists in a world beyond that. His success is of his own doing.

Fair enough, Warner had the wisdom to allow him to control his artistic process, but it took brain power and real ambition for Prince to do what he did. It didn't take a well-oiled machine to feed him ideas, saying 'Do your hair like this' or 'Ride a motorcycle here.' That is all him. He is a product of his own imagination.

PASTRY

IN THE WORDS OF MICHAEL VAN HUFFEL

"There was always chaos when it came to accounts. Prince could fire accountants from reputable agencies if they told him things needed to change or that he was spending money on facilities he wasn't using. Staffing at Paisley Park would go from eighty down to five, depending on how Prince was feeling and how much money he wanted to spend.

During one of the overblown periods, he hired a pastry chef from New York. He didn't really eat pastry, so it made about as much sense as a regular person having a zeppelin hangar. This chef moved to Minneapolis to bake pastries that no one ate.

So the story goes: he fired his accountant and figured he needed a replacement more than he needed croissants on the regular. Prince called his pastry chef into a meeting and asked her to do his accounts. She explained she wasn't qualified, so he asked her: 'Dollars, cents, teaspoons, what's the difference?' This woman had given up a great job in New York to move to Minnesota and make pies for no reason.

Everyone knew accounting wasn't her thing. A member of the band, who shall remain nameless, wanted to talk about his paycheck. The pastry-accountant woman said, 'If you need something from accounting, you have to come to me,' to which he responded, 'Thanks, but I'll come to you if I need a tray of cookies.'"

LEFT *On stage as ♂ during the Ultimate Live Experience tour, Brabanthallen, Den Bosch, The Netherlands, March 24, 1995.*

COUNT THE DAYS

IN THE WORDS OF MICHAEL VAN HUFFEL

"He said he didn't believe in time. There is a fundamental truth in that. He didn't live by any kind of clock. He lived more lives than anybody I know, mostly because he didn't sleep.

My theory on him is he grew up abandoned and abused and teased in school. Through force of will, talent, and drive and a metabolism that should've been studied by doctors, he created a world in which he was the opposite of the kid people made fun of. He was short, so he thought, 'Fuck it, I'll wear heels. I'm geeky. Fuck that, I'll be the sexiest person you've ever seen in your life.' For better or worse, he built this insulated world that was his. If you were pulled into his orbit, it was a different set of physics.

His charisma and intellect were a reality distortion field. He was seductive. He'd talk you into doing something and you'd think, 'This is great!' It was like hypnosis. You'd leave and think, 'What the fuck did I just agree to? I can't do that.' It forced you to be the very best version of yourself you could be. Aside from the terror and likelihood of ulcers, it meant that he believed in you.

It was winter. I was in bed and my phone started ringing. 'Michael, can you come in?' I looked out the window and shuddered. I could see what felt like six feet of snow and my frozen car. 'I've just finished this song and I'd like you to hear it. I want you to do something to match it visually.' He knew the power of inviting us into the studio. He knew it was special, but that didn't change the fact it was the middle of the night. I paused and then said, 'You know, I can come in early tomorrow?' Silence. And then: 'Are you coming?'

I scraped the ice off my windscreen and headed to Paisley. It was just us in the building. I think it was Studio C. The one near the front door. He played it to me, 'Count the Days.' I thought it was extraordinarily beautiful. I was genuinely moved and really excited. We walked to the office and, while I was firing up my computer, he was carrying on and on saying, 'People are gonna be tripping when they hear how much I swore in this song!' Really? He channeled this gorgeousness but all he could talk about was the swearing? I thought, 'Do you even know what you just did?'

We talked through a few ideas. He wanted a Salvador Dali–style melting clock. He wanted to see a finished record cover with a title and everything. Within a day or two he made me send it out. There was so much to fix, but he wanted it out. He liked the physical product. He liked to imagine it in a store. He liked to imagine someone seeing it and wanting it."

ABOVE On stage as ⚦ during the Ultimate Live Experience tour, Brabanthallen, Den Bosch, The Netherlands, March 24, 1995.

WHILE BATTLING WITH HIS RECORD COMPANY, ♔ TAKES ON ANOTHER ALTER EGO: TORA TORA—A JAPANESE WAR CRY MEANING "LIGHTNING ATTACK."

THE MISSING JAW HARP

IN THE WORDS OF ANGELO MOORE, LEAD SINGER, FISHBONE

"He showed up to watch a Fishbone show at Elysée Montmartre in Paris. I could see his face way in the back on the balcony. It was years later, in 1995, that one of his people got in touch and asked me to come to a rehearsal. They were gonna be on a TV show and he wanted me to play with the band.

The day I met him, he was wearing a green veil over his face. He was doing that Tora Tora thing at the time. He didn't talk much. I thought the veil was just some art shit. He was not the kind of motherfucker to do that for a show. He was that person all the time. He was authentic.

So we rehearsed for the White Room in London. We flew over and he asked me to put on a mask for the show. It was a harlequin thing. Porcelain I think. I played soprano saxophone on 'Big Fun.'

After the taping, we went to a party. I said, 'Hey man, check this out.' I played my jaw harp for him and said, 'You try it.' He took it and walked out the door. He never came back. That's the last time I ever saw him.

'Big Fun' was cut out of the show. A few months later, he sampled my song 'Lyin'ass Bitch' on his record. He didn't ask permission and we didn't get paid, but I thought, 'Fine, he felt like a sample of my voice was good enough to convey what he wanted.' I was OK with it. I would have liked my jaw harp back, though."

OPPOSITE *As Tora Tora at a record signing, Virgin Megastore, London, 1995.*

CARTOON KITTY CAT

IN THE WORDS OF MICHAEL VAN HUFFEL

"There were *so* many different remixes of 'Pussy Control.' I remember I made a logo that looked like a cartoon kitty-cat head. We had buttons and T-shirts made. It was funny seeing Duane, Prince's brother, wearing that button over his three-piece suit.

One of the 'Pussy Control' remixes had a bunch of Beavis and Butthead samples in it. The main sample was one of the characters yelling 'vagina!' over and over again. There was a video, too; mostly a bunch of porn clips cut together with that sort of old-style video mirror effect throughout. I don't think any of that stuff actually came out."

FREE MUSIC

IN THE WORDS OF MICHAEL BLAND

"Prince was always wanting to put out more music. He felt the work he was doing was very relevant at the time. He didn't want to wait to put it out. Any artist, if you're a sculptor or a painter or whatever, you want to show off your work and have instant gratification. It's the same thing.

We'd recorded *Come* and *The Gold Experience* simultaneously. We didn't know what songs would be on what album or what the record would be called. You put out one record and then go to the record company straight after with another one and, of course, they say, 'No!'

In 1995, we were touring with *The Gold Experience,* even though the album wasn't out. People show up. They want to hear the hits and we're not giving them any! There were a lot of people upset about that.

He got bored with his catalog. A real artist has to grow and evolve. It can't be like a circus with the same guy juggling stuff and the same guy sticking things in the lion's mouth. It gets tiresome. Like any real artist, you want to expand and change and that's not what your audience wants of you. They want you to keep recycling the same stuff.

He said to me one time, 'You don't know what it means to be on a hit tour with a hit movie, playing the same 'Purple Rain' guitar solo the exact same way ninety-one times in a row. If you change one thing, people go crazy.' It was torture for him to have to do things the same way every night."

RIGHT On stage as ♀ at an undated performance consisting almost entirely of new, unreleased material.

really huge. A giant vagina on one side and in the center was what we'd call the womb. That contained the soundboard.

It looked amazing, but I remember one of the crew saying the set was 'for a music video, not for a concert.' It was almost impossible to move around. The tour wasn't selling out by any means, so we started leaving bits of the set behind. It was a cost-cutting thing. By the time we got to Scotland, we only had the womb left.

There was a dark cloud hanging over us from the record company politics. All the interviews and press were about that. It's like being at war. We did a stop-off in Brussels while we were in transit. He got the crowd to chant 'Prince is dead!'

There were aftershows pretty much every night. I remember playing tambourine on 'The Cross' while Bono did guest vocals in Dublin. I was a young man, so it was exciting for me, but I think we were barely covering costs. A new accountant was brought in and started cutting corners. A lot of the tech people had to share rooms. **"**

THIS IS NEVER GOING TO HAPPEN

IN THE WORDS OF FAFU

" We got called into a meeting. He said, 'We need ideas on how to make money.' He mentioned that Sonny and Michael had put together a sample CD with some of their own music. They were called Funky Ass Loops and Smooth Grooves. I jumped in and said, 'Yeah, I put that together for them. Do you want to make a sample CD?' He responded, 'Well, I want to make some money.'

I spent the next few weeks going through his back catalog and picking out anything I thought hip-hop artists might want to sample. I even went through *The Time* albums. I made the CD with a ton of notes and gave it to him. He called me later that day, 'The first thing you have to do is call Warner Brothers and get them to sign off on this.' I was the drum programmer, man! I was barely twenty at the time, so I thought, 'What am I supposed to do with this?' I passed it on to one of his assistants, who just said something like, 'This is never going to happen.' And that was the last I ever heard of it. "

THE RADIO IN HIS HEAD

IN THE WORDS OF MICHAEL VAN HUFFEL

"Prince would listen to odd new-age music. I would hear environmental records and Enya-style stuff. You know that kind of 'flute guy' Yanni? That kind of thing. It's like almost comical new-age music. It's just my guess, but I think it would help to turn off the radio in his head."

KAMASUTRA

IN THE WORDS OF BRENT FISCHER

"We would get music from him. I would transcribe it and my father would write the arrangement. I would assist him and towards the end of his life I became his cowriter and then ghost writer. I like to think the writing of [American composer and keyboardist] Clare Fischer had an effect on Prince's writing over the years.

Prince purchased a Synclavier in the '90s. It was the closest thing to a sampled orchestra that existed at the time. He sent us a piece that was very much orchestrally motivated. He wanted some of the music duplicated with live orchestra.

Transcribing that took a lot of time, because he had recorded onto a forty-eight-track digital tape. It was difficult to hear everything that was on there. I transcribed a lot of it track by track. I was on tour at the time, so, with a Walkman, I transcribed on planes, trains, buses, and whenever I would find the time. I faxed back the transcripts to my father and he started work on it in L.A. I believe it was called *Kamasutra*."

ABOVE *On stage during the Ultimate Live Experience*
tour, 1995.

THE DAY ⚥ MARRIED MAYTE

IN THE WORDS OF FAFU

" The wedding was pretty tiny, at a small church in South Minneapolis. There were perhaps forty people there in total and apart from Prince and Mayte, I didn't really know anyone. We had a kind of marquee constructed to cover the front of the church so the awaiting paparazzi couldn't get any pictures. Prince was dropped off at the back of the church in a delivery van.

I remember Prince's parents, sister, and his brother, Duane, were all there. The band weren't invited. I was only there because it was my job to cue the music. I was given a program and told when to press play, fade down, and fade up again at the end. We brought across a small PA system and a CD he'd burned called *Kamasutra*. The idea was I'd hit play when they walked down the aisle. I guess I'd gained his trust by then. Mavis Staples came up to me afterward and said, 'The music sounded beautiful.'

The reception was back at Paisley Park in the atrium. I was entrusted with the music again and I was hanging out in the backroom. I was so hungry, so I asked the caterers for food. They said, 'We have to serve everyone first.' At one point, I came out of the front door in the middle of the atrium. Prince's table was in the hallway. He waved me over and said, 'Did you eat? Have a seat.' "

ABOVE On stage with Mayte during the Ultimate Live Experience tour, Brabanthallen, Den Bosch, The Netherlands, March 24, 1995.

OPPOSITE ⚥ performs 'Dinner with Delores' on NBC News Today, July 9, 1996.

WHO HE IS

IN THE WORDS OF RHONDA SMITH, BASS, INTERMITTENTLY, 1996–2009

" We were in New York. It was the first TV show I did with him. It was *Letterman,* promoting *Chaos and Disorder*. We played 'Dinner with Delores.' We were only there for two days, but he hired a studio and wanted to cut stuff. Meshell Ndegeocello was with us. We went back and forth on some tunes.

He's a constant creator. It's a different game when you're dealing with an anomaly like that. That's just who he is. Every session was a great opportunity. It's in history. I'm not waiting for anything more we recorded to be released. If it comes out, that's fantastic. If not that's OK, too. I have some very nice memories. "

A PIECE OF PLUTONIUM

IN THE WORDS OF MICHAEL VAN HUFFEL

I came into work one day. His wife Mayte came to my office and handed me a CD jewel case. She said, 'He wants you to have this.'

It was a full package, so to speak. That is, a cover, insert, art behind where the CD sits, and the back. The cover was an image of him that I was mocking up for the *Emancipation* album. In the part where the CD sits, there were somewhat meticulous patterns drawn in pen. There was a CD inside with the songs, none of which had been released.

My first thought was Prince had put this together as a basis for something he wanted me to make into fully realized album artwork. If it was a project he wanted me to do, I wanted to get on it. He would want to see progress.

I called Therese. Therese was, at the time, sort of Prince's right-hand person. I liked her. She'd been around for a long time, had a very strong personality, was somewhat jaded, and very easily annoyed. I said, 'Do you know what this CD package is about?' The response: 'All I know is that he drove us crazy last night, sending people out to get scissors, glue, markers. In his office this morning, he cut up a bunch of really expensive coffee-table photo books and there's a huge mess I had to clean up.' I said, 'Oh. Do you know what it's for?' And she said something along the lines of, 'It's a gift, dummy.'

I stared at this thing. Having a CD of unreleased music felt like I had a piece of plutonium. I had it on my desk and I kept looking over at it, still baffled.

Later that day, he came in to tell me what to work on. I picked up the CD and I said 'So, er, Mayte gave this to me this morning.' He nodded and said, 'It's for you.' I said, 'Thanks, man.' He shook his head, which I took to mean 'Be quiet now.' He looked at me for a second and then split.

That night I listened to the CD. It was all new music. It was really exciting. I kept thinking he'd likely ask me for it back. He never did. I never found out exactly why he did that. I think it was a bit of a gratitude thing, a moment of real generosity. Most of those songs eventually came out in one form or another. It's not extraordinary in itself, it's a collage of images glued together and handwriting and squiggles. But it is something extraordinary and one of the few possessions I care about. It is entirely unique.

OPPOSITE Handmade CD package by ♀, featuring
an early track list for Emancipation.

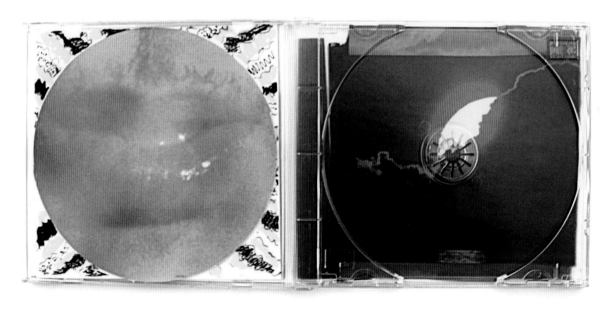

FEBRUARY 1996 ♀ EXPLAINS: "PRINCE IS THE NAME THAT MY MOTHER GAVE ME AT BIRTH. WARNER BROTHERS TOOK THE NAME AND USED IT AS THE MAIN MARKETING TOOL TO PROMOTE ALL OF THE MUSIC THAT I WROTE. IN THE BEGINNING, BOTH YOUTH AND EXCITEMENT TOWARD THE OPPORTUNITY TO HAVE AN ALBUM PRODUCED MADE ME, AS PRINCE, NAIVE. SAVVY LAWYERS CLAIMING TO HAVE MY INTERESTS AT HEART, LONG IN BED WITH THE RECORD COMPANIES THEY PIMP, OFFERED ME WHAT SEEMED TO BE A LUCRATIVE CONTRACT, WITHOUT FULLY EXPLAINING THE RAMIFICATIONS OF ITS TERMS.

I WROTE AN ALBUM A YEAR FOR MANY YEARS UNTIL I REALIZED A TRAP HAD BEEN LAID. I WOULD NEVER BE ABLE TO LEAVE THE LEGACY OF MY MUSIC TO MY FAMILY, MY FUTURE CHILDREN, OR ANYONE, BECAUSE 'PRINCE' DID NOT OWN THE MASTERS—I DID NOT, AND STILL DO NOT, OWN MY ART."

DAYS AFTER LEAVING THE RECORD CONTRACT HE ENTERED AS A TEENAGER, ♀ DECLARES NOVEMBER 19, 1996 "EMANCIPATION DAY." HE RELEASES THE ALBUM *EMANCIPATION* THROUGH EMI RECORDS AND DESCRIBES THE THREE-HOUR SET AS THE ALBUM HE WAS "BORN TO MAKE."

THE TRUTH

IN THE WORDS OF HANS-MARTIN BUFF, SOUND ENGINEER 1996–2000

"I had come into the fold when he was making *Emancipation*. There were a ton of engineers and a lot of that stuff was already done when I arrived. You hear my voice on the song 'Joint 2 Joint,' where I play a taxi driver, but I had my eyes on something more. I wanted to make an entire album with him.

It was winter 1996 and *Emancipation* was about to come out. He was really into Ani DiFranco, so he wanted to make an acoustic album. He played 'The Truth' and 'Don't Play Me' just like you hear them on the album. The gap is exactly the same and he did both songs from start to finish in one take. He added some effects afterward, but these songs were done, just like that. Then there were the heartfelt songs like 'Comeback' and its introduction 'Mindblow.' It was just four lines long. A reflection on loss. For whatever reason, he cut it.

He decided he wanted to write some stuff with his bassist Rhonda Smith. She played him a cassette with six riffs/chord progressions. Right in front of me, he would add to what she had written and sketch out a song. That's how 'Man in a Uniform' and '3rdeye' came to be.

A few months later. On the weekend of Easter '97, the drummer David 'Fingers' Haynes was in town to jam with Prince. I think he'd been recommended by Rhonda. I remember labeling those sessions 'Jams One to Six' and putting them in the vault. David never became part of the band, but something they worked on became the song 'Fascination.' Prince wanted to strip it back to fit with the acoustic feel of *The Truth* album, so the only thing that remained from those sessions was David's kick drum. It's on 'Fascination,' uncredited."

OPPOSITE ♀ *in Canada, December 1996.*

MIND BLOW
IN THE WORDS OF STEVE PARKE

" I was used to Prince responding to conversations, happenings, life, by creating new music. 'Welcome 2 the Dawn' was recorded in response to a photograph I'd taken of him. It took a few hours. I was used to him working fast.

One morning, at about five, we were talking through some stuff and he was messing with his guitar. I must have been feeling brave, because I said, 'I think most people overlook your vocal arrangements. It's lost on people.' He gave me a nod.

The next day he called me down to the studio. There were candles everywhere. He told me to have a seat and he hit play. It was acapella. Just layers and layers of vocals. My jaw hit the floor. I remember the lines: 'It's so quiet I can hear my hair grow. I can feel my mind blow.' It was incredibly personal. It ended and I was floored. Leaving the studio, I thought, 'I will try to hold onto this for as long as I can.' I knew in that moment it would never make it to release. I looked at it as a song about isolation. It's as if he would put things out there that were really bare but then flinch and think, 'I don't want to do this yet.' **"**

BELOW *Guest pass for the Jam of the Year tour, July 1997–January 1998.*

CHINESE DRAGON-DOGS AND PLASTIC PALM TREES

IN THE WORDS OF KIMBER LAWLER, ART DIRECTOR, 1997–1998

" He wanted a Paisley Park revamp. The first job was to toss up clouds all over the walls in the atrium. I painted a mural of a waterfall and that became the artwork for the 'The Holy River' single.

Next thing, we went on the tour. In Toronto, I was told I needed to construct a set. There was really no time at all. I don't know anything about Toronto. I called a prop rental place and hired in a bunch of stuff. I'm talking plastic palm trees and gold Chinese dragon-dogs. They were made of plaster with a little metal wire holding them together. Everything had to be ostentatious. He liked things you can imagine Marie Antoinette throwing up.

He said, 'Buy the dogs and palm trees. We're taking them on the road.' There were no cases or anything, because they were meant for hire. It was so makeshift. At one of the shows, I almost had a heart attack when he climbed up on the dog. I thought, 'Holy shit! It's held together by a few coat hangers!'

I would often put something on set, knowing it was dreadful, just so he would remove it. Like an orange grandma shawl over the piano. It was bait. It gave him control. It was chaotic. It was stressful, but it was also a privilege. I learned a lot. He was great to me most of the time. "

OPPOSITE *Arriving at Life Cafe for a*   **ABOVE LEFT** *On stage during the Jam*

GOD

IN THE WORDS OF LARRY GRAHAM, BASS, SLY AND THE FAMILY STONE/ GRAHAM CENTRAL STATION

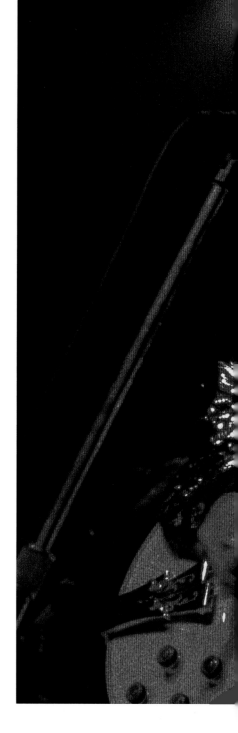

" It was 1997. My band Graham Central Station was playing alongside Teena Marie and Earth Wind and Fire in Nashville, and on the same night Prince was in town playing a bigger venue. We were invited to the aftershow. I ended up on stage playing with Prince's band. He thought it was funny that my wife carried my guitar pedal in her handbag.

A few months later, he sent me one of his new releases in the mail. In return, I sent a book called *You Can Live Forever in Paradise on Earth*. He called me and asked if he could make seven copies for the members of his band. I told him I'd bring him some books myself and we met up again in New York.

I didn't know back then, but he really liked my music. He asked me if my band would open for him on tour. Every night, after the shows we would get together and talk about the Bible. Just before the tour ended, he asked if I'd think about moving to Minnesota to continue teaching him the Bible.

We started off with one-on-one study. Then he came to Kingdom Hall, sometimes three times a week, for group discussions. The more knowledge you gain, the more you want to dedicate your life to Jehovah and that's what he did. Baptism is a public declaration of that. When Prince was baptized, I was with him. It was a joyous day. If there are things you need to start or stop doing, you follow through. He made the adjustments he needed to make. He dedicated his life to God.

I was raised as an only child, but Prince became part of my family. He was my spiritual brother and he became my brother in flesh, too. We used to go bowling, watch movies, eat dinner, or just hang out with the family. He was a regular person with a great heart.

He never forgot about my wife carrying my guitar pedal in a bag. He would tell that story all the time. "

" HE ASKED IF I'D THINK ABOUT MOVING TO MINNESOTA TO CONTINUE TEACHING HIM THE BIBLE. " *LARRY GRAHAM*

ABOVE *On stage with Larry Graham, Irving Plaza, New York City, April 11, 1998.*

CRYSTAL BALL

IN THE WORDS OF HANS-MARTIN BUFF

" He gave me a list of songs and I had to find them. We went into the fabled vault. It looks like a basement room with a wheel on the door. It's probably twice the size of your living room. It starts from the left and it has rows and rows of tapes that are chronologically labeled. On the right is the newest stuff. There's a computer and a cataloging system.

Someone was with me to make sure I didn't take anything home. I emerged with a stack of tapes that I'd not heard before. We put them together. Edited a lot. Cut a lot. There was little mixing. The whole process took two weeks. And there we had *Crystal Ball*. Bootlegs were out and that pissed him off. He wanted control over what he was saying and how he was saying it.

There were some choices I would have made differently, but that applied to other projects, too. *New Power Soul* could have been a harder funk album. *Rave* could have been a rock album. It's not as simple as saying, 'Did he put the best stuff out?' Everyone I've ever worked with has wanted my opinion, except for Prince. He once joked, 'The day Hans says, "You can do better than that" is the day he gets fired.'

Some of the songs on *Crystal Ball* were considered outtake-outtakes by fans. He said what he wanted to say with it. Putting out what others might consider 'the very best' would be like ending the sentence. There's a quote: 'An artist does not arrive anywhere. It's a constant state of becoming.' I think Prince had figured that out. "

LEFT ⚥ *in silhouette, performing "The Holy River" at the VH1 Honours, April 10, 1997.*

CHAOS AND $11,000,000

IN THE WORDS OF JACQUI THOMPSON, MANAGER/PRESIDENT OF NPG RECORDS, 1996–2000

" Prince needed someone to manage 1-800-New-Funk, a merchandise hotline that allowed him to sell merchandise directly to fans. I was working from an office at Paisley Park, answering the phone and taking orders. It was my voice on the 1-800-New-Funk voicemail and it was even sampled for a remix of 'Face Down' that never came out.

Prince wanted everything, and I mean everything, to be done in-house. He decided he wanted to work outside the industry. He wanted to sell the *Crystal Ball* set directly to fans by taking preorders over the phone. He said, 'Why do I have to sell three million copies to get a tiny share from a record company when I can make the same cash selling a fraction to fans directly?' It was an experiment in being an independent artist.

I suggested we outsource the shipping. I gave him options, but ultimately he would decide what he wanted to do and he decided to keep things in-house. It was chaos. The ordering system was designed without dates, so you couldn't see when orders had been placed. Some fans got the album months later than they should have. Others were double charged. We got some bad press and eventually he agreed to get some outside help.

He felt he had earned the right to do things on his terms and financially at least, it worked. He sold 250,000 copies through the hotline and made $11,000,000. He wanted other artists to step outside the system, too. "

LEFT *On stage during the* New Power Soul *tour, 1998.*

IMPLEMENTATION WAS THE PROBLEM

IN THE WORDS OF STEVE PARKE

"He was always excited by concepts. Implementation was the problem. *The Gold Experience* was meant to have a gold foil cover, but Warner Brothers said it was too expensive. *The Crystal Ball* set was meant to be an actual translucent ball with the discs floating inside, but it would cost so much to ship. We ended up with something that looked like a see-through hockey puck.

I planned for *New Power Soul* to be printed on black flock paper so it would look like a retro black-light poster. It would have taken a little time, but I remember him saying, 'People are waiting for this album.' I wasn't happy with the finished artwork. We rushed them through and the albums sat in a warehouse for six months.

He would never stop engaging. I remember him doing a late-night party in the atrium of Paisley Park. He was perhaps twenty feet away. He strolled over to me while he was playing a key-tar and spoke into my ear, 'I like the stuff you put together today, but let's talk through how we take it forward.' He's in the middle of a keyboard solo and I'm having a ball, yet he just doesn't stop talking shop. He never switched off.

Even when we were busting a gut, our employer was always working harder. It's difficult to be creative on the spot, but he could be, so it became an aspiration for everyone around him. There was a lot of respect, even in the moments when we might have wanted to say, 'Fuck you.'"

ABOVE *At Paisley Park sound stage, July 1998.*

OPPOSITE *With Chaka Khan, on stage during the* New Power Soul *tour, 1998.*

WOMEN

IN THE WORDS OF JACQUI THOMPSON

"We were working on a TV special and the channel made some suggestions about who could interview him. He wanted Mel B from the Spice Girls. She flew out to Paisley Park. They had a childlike connection. I know he thought she was cute. Rosario Dawson was another one. She came to Paisley to record some spoken word stuff. He really liked women and feminine energy. It's not just a sexual thing. He was just very comfortable around women."

DIY

IN THE WORDS OF JACQUI THOMPSON

"He didn't like titles, so he wouldn't give me one. Colleagues would say, 'You're managing him' and eventually Prince said, 'You're the president of NPG Records.' It was so DIY, I booked him onto *The Jay Leno Show*. I was organizing his tours, calling T-shirt manufacturers, and trying to manage PR.

He had me make a video for the song 'Come On.' We were on the road in London. He said, 'Get a beta crew and meet me in Hyde Park.' We had no permits. We were shooting on some kind of camcorder. It was meant to look crappy and homemade. He jumps out of the limo wearing a fake beard and a flat cap, disguised as an old dude, and starts talking to strangers. We filmed him saying, 'I've got the butter for your muffin,' a line from the song, to hot girls like some old pervert. They had no idea who they were talking to.

I was in the edit, too. Every time I thought, 'That's not my area,' he'd talk me round. I ended up doing a whole bunch of stuff I never expected to do."

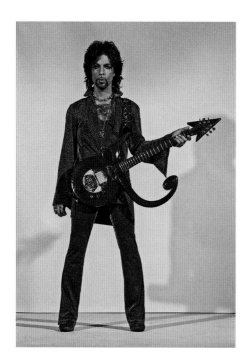

LEFT Promo still for the Mill City Music Festival, Minneapolis, April 1999.

OPPOSITE Promo still taken during the filming of "The Greatest Romance Ever Sold" video shoot.

OLD FRIENDS FOR SALE

IN THE WORDS OF MICHAEL BLAND

" Years earlier there was talk of a movie, *I'll Do Anything,* with Nick Nolte and Julie Kavner. Prince was supposed to score the movie and his songs were supposed to be in it. Then they told him that the woman who plays the voice of Marge Simpson would be singing his songs. He said, 'No way. I don't want Marge Simpson singing my music!' That was the end of that. Lots of that stuff eventually came out on the album *Old Friends for Sale*. Marge wasn't on that record either. "

IT IS 1999. AFTER RELEASING *CRYSTAL BALL* AS AN INDEPENDENT ARTIST, ⚥ ENLISTS THE HELP OF CLIVE DAVIS, PRESIDENT OF ARISTA RECORDS, FOR HIS NEXT MAJOR LABEL RELEASE.

ABOVE *Standing in front of his purple prowler, Chanhassen Arboretum, October 1999.*

RAVE UN2 THE JOY FANTASTIC

IN THE WORDS OF HANS-MARTIN BUFF

"There were three mini albums that evolved into *Rave*. Stuff like *Madrid 2 Chicago* featured 'Man O' War.' They were love songs. There was funky rock stuff like 'So Far, So Pleased.' That was originally a duet with Marva King, not Gwen Stefani. There was a hard rock cover of 'Still the One' by Shania Twain. Some of this stuff was released via the NPG Music Club, his online outlet, but a lot of it changed shape and became *Rave Un2 the Joy Fantastic*.

He was inspired by Santana's comeback at the time. He wanted the album to be a hit. We would hear whispers from the press. I remember someone at Paisley asking, 'Are you guys working with a producer?' He had put something online about bringing in his 'favorite producer from the '80s.' We didn't know what to think but it turned out his 'favorite producer' was Prince. He was consciously going for a retro sound.

We took out the LinnDrum machine from the basement. I'm talking about the same one he used in the '80s. I got it repaired. He showed me how it worked with a lot of pride. Like most things, he used it like you're not supposed to. He would put guitar pedals behind the toms and create those weird fills you get on tunes like 'The Ballad of Dorothy Parker.' The result was the song 'Strange but True.' The original is eight minutes-something.

Every day, we would upgrade the sequence we were working on. That's how the album grew. He became hesitant about 'Strange but True,' I suspect because the lyrics were so personal. By that point, I was good friends with Manuela, who was working at Paisley (she later become Prince's wife), so we spoke when he wasn't around and we formed an alliance to save 'Strange but True.' That's the kind of thing only he can do. I suggested we cut 'The Sun, The Moon and Stars.' In my mind, it was a little corny. He laughed and asked, 'Hans, how's your sex life?'

There's a segue which was originally the voice of Miles Davis saying, 'Prince, Prince, Prince, Prince.' It was taken from an interview in which Miles said, 'Prince is as good as any jazz musician.' Of course, that pleased Prince, but the Davis estate wouldn't allow clearance, so it was replaced by four seconds of silence 'dedicated to Miles.'

There were a bunch of songs that he 'made to order,' too. He explained, 'I need a song for your mom.' That's how 'Silly Game' and 'The Greatest Romance Ever Sold' came into being. I said, 'That's not what my mom would listen to, but I understand you.'

'The Greatest Romance' was the lead single and there were a lot of promotional plans from Arista. Clive Davis took the whole thing very personally. He would call the studio to ask for changes, but a lot of the time Prince wouldn't take his calls. I'd pick up and Prince would wave at me and tell me to pretend he wasn't available.

I'm a shitkicker from Germany and I had one of the pillars of the music industry talking to me on the phone, begging me to change a song. I'd want to say, 'Clive, you need to understand, I'm only talking to you because Prince doesn't want to.'

On one occasion, Prince eventually grabbed the phone and Clive asked him about having 'The Greatest Romance' remixed. Prince calmly responded, 'OK, Clive, I understand. I'd rather be dragged through nails.'"

THE GREATEST ROMANCE EVER SOLD

IN THE WORDS OF STEVE PARKE

" This is poignant to me. I was doing a photo shoot for *The Truth* album with Prince wearing a pinstripe suit. He was noodling blues licks and ad libbing vocals. It was straightforward, pure blues. He was playing while I took pictures. I said, 'When are you going to put out an album like that?' He responded, 'When I get old.'

Jump forward a couple of years to 1999 and the release of *Rave Un2 the Joy Fantastic*. He's in full pop-star mode again and I'm taking pictures at the video shoot for the single 'The Greatest Romance Ever Sold.' It's just my hunch, but the fact that we were doing the video after the single had gone to radio tells me that it wasn't a priority. He would do several takes. He was ready to roll all the time, but it was not a fun process for him. It was not the first thing on his mind.

I always hoped he could relax into himself, but there were times when he would work to live up to expectations. I was taking pictures of him sat at a table. In a quiet moment, he said, 'I don't like doing this. It's hard. My skin has to be perfect and I have to look a particular way.' He looked around the room at his staff and all the crew and explained, 'It's hard to know that I'm responsible for these people's livelihoods. They have kids and families.'

I got the impression that if he wasn't the superstar we know, he would be playing in bars and doing a regular nine-to-five to support his music making. When I was in the studio with him, he was always having fun. That is where his brain and heart were most comfortable. At those big arena shows and on video shoots, I thought he was always a bit like 'I have to do this again?'

That's why he was always making the next record. He was always in the studio making more music. "

OPPOSITE Still taken during "The Greatest Romance Ever Sold" video shoot.

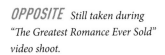

THE ELUSIVE CHANTEUSE SHOWS UP AT PAISLEY PARK

IN THE WORDS OF HANS-MARTIN BUFF

" Mariah Carey had started work on the '80s throwback musical *Glitter*. She came to Paisley Park, complete with a caricature entourage. They had a wonderful air of importance about them. I remember Prince and I in the studio shooting each other looks and thinking, 'Is that what superstars are really like?' Prince had written a song 'Vavoom' with a distinct '80s vibe. He played it to Mariah and her entourage for consideration. Mariah didn't look impressed and she never covered the song. "

OPPOSITE Swimming at his home in Marbella, Spain, June 1999.

LEFT On the sound stage at Paisley Park Studios, April 1999.

BLACK PEOPLE LOVE CHICKEN

IN THE WORDS OF SAM JENNINGS, WEB DESIGNER/ART DIRECTOR, 1998–2008

" I'd already worked on his charity website www.love4oneanother.com, but in 2000 we started having business meetings with Microsoft to figure out some kind of music distribution partnership. Prince wanted the direct connection with fans. A clear channel with no record company or middleman.

For everything that made it to the website, there were five ideas from Prince that didn't work. We had to explain bandwidth to him and the limits of the Internet at the time. He was wildly ambitious and he has a charisma, which means you do your absolute best. He wanted a virtual house where the subscribers could come together. A virtual place of higher consciousness. To get to the house and look around, you had to click through images of space with statements flying through the galaxy. It was a call and response thing:

The earth is flat—The earth is a unique sphere
All that glitters is not gold—On prom night who cares?
Black people love chicken—U mean it doesn't really taste good?

The idea was you have to get past assumption and norms to find a new world. More than anything, it was a way to get music to people outside of the industry model. "

OPPOSITE On the sound stage at Paisley Park Studios, April 1999.

ON MAY 16, 2000, ALMOST SEVEN YEARS AFTER BECOMING ♀,
HE ANNOUNCES HE WILL RECLAIM HIS BIRTH NAME, PRINCE.
"I WILL NOW GO BACK TO USING MY NAME INSTEAD OF THE
SYMBOL I ADOPTED AS A MEANS TO FREE MYSELF FROM
UNDESIRABLE RELATIONSHIPS."

THE RAINBOW CHILDREN

IN THE WORDS OF NAJEE, SAXOPHONE AND FLUTE, 2000–2003

" He said, 'I'd like you to record an album with me.' He told me it was called *The Rainbow Children*. He was looking for a new direction. He brought in John Blackwell to play drums. He's a finessed, technical drummer. He bought in Renato Neto, a virtuoso keys player. He brought me in because of my jazz background. It's clear to me that Prince was searching.

The basic tracks were already recorded. As a natural jazz player who improvises a lot, I could have taken it to many places, but Prince knew exactly what he wanted. There was no engineer. Just Prince and I. He would sing the parts he wanted me to play. I would write out a chart and play flute to mimic what he sung. Honestly, when I heard the record, I didn't remember playing a lot of that stuff. Prince is like a painter and only he knows what the finished picture will be.

That kind of record is not for radio. He didn't care about that. It was a personal statement. I equate that record with Miles Davis' *Bitches Brew*. There was a desire to break away, whether his audience accepted it or not. In my opinion, it was way left of what his audience came to expect. A lot of people didn't get it. The ones like that end up being the most treasured records in history. "

OPPOSITE On the sound stage at
Paisley Park Studios, October 1999.

THE GLORY OF GOD

IN THE WORDS OF SAM JENNINGS

" In early 2001, Prince called me down to the studio, handed me a lyric book, and played his new album *The Rainbow Children* to me from start to finish. He stood right there for the whole thing. I said, 'You've been saving your best for something like this.' That's not to say the stuff that came before was bad, but *The Rainbow Children* was a complete project, different from all the individual disconnected songs that came out in the years before.

He wanted to make a big statement about becoming a Jehovah's Witness and getting baptized. A big part of the faith is getting other people to participate. If you were around him, eventually he would talk to you about Bible study. I grew up in an atheist household, so I had no preconceptions about God. He would get so lively and animated. I never felt intimidated or pressured. It was actually kinda fun.

Everything was a devotional act to him at that time. The performing and the music was all for the glory of God in his mind. I felt the sincerity of that. "

ONE NITE ALONE...

IN THE WORDS OF NAJEE

" The *One Nite Alone . . .* tour was focused completely on music, more so than those big arena shows. We played small theaters and backstage Prince ran a sterile atmosphere. One time, George Clinton came over. I remember him joking, 'I can't be back here with ya'll. There's no women, no nothing!'

Prince was completely focused. Just like the studio sessions, he would sing the parts he wanted me to play and I would write them out, rehearse, and play. We'd sound check from four p.m., do the show from eight-thirty p.m., then shower and head to the aftershow. Prince would film almost every show and then ask me to watch it back. I would be falling asleep on his couch. He'd say, 'Najee! Look at what you played!' Honestly, I never saw Prince sleep. "

LEFT *On stage performing 'The Everlasting Now' on* The Tonight Show *with Jay Leno, December 13, 2002.*

N.E.W.S

IN THE WORDS OF ERIC LEEDS

"Around 2002, Prince came to a club show I was playing. We hadn't seen each other or spoken for years. I ended up playing with his band for a few sporadic dates. *The One Nite Alone . . .* tour was one of the nicest things I'd ever done with him. It was mostly new music and he was playing it because he enjoyed it. It felt like he was content, not chasing the arena money or selling out stadiums.

N.E.W.S was just one of those spontaneous things he does. I can say the total amount of time it took to make the album was the duration of the finished record. It was probably mixed as we recorded it.

The band were in Studio B at Paisley. I was in an iso booth and everyone else was in the main room. Prince had a talk-back mic that didn't go to tape. It just went into our headphones. He said, 'Here is the key, here is the groove, start to play.' We'd be in D minor for 5 minutes and he'd say, 'Go to F,' or 'Eric, start the solo.' It was that simple."

RIGHT *All access pass to the* One Nite Alone . . . *tour, March–November 2002.*

THE 46TH ANNUAL GRAMMY AWARDS
IN THE WORDS OF BRENT FISCHER

"Early 2004, Prince's office got in touch. We were told he had a song for us to work on that would open the 46th Grammy awards. We were sent a CD starting off with 'Purple Rain' and running into a medley. My father, Prince, and I had a conference call. He had some specific requests. He wanted a rhythmic element of the medley mimicked by the orchestra. He gave us freedom to get as granular as we wanted with the arrangement.

By this point, I was cowriting with my father. He would write all day and put his pencil down when he was tired, even if it was in the middle of a phrase. I'd pick up and work through the night and we would repeat that cycle, until it was done.

We didn't know until the dress rehearsal that the medley featured Beyoncé. On the CD he sent, Prince was doing the Beyoncé vocal. He covers 'Crazy in Love' as authentically as you can imagine. The performance was a triumph. He thanked me and my father profusely. It was just wonderful."

OPPOSITE With Beyoncé, on stage at the 46th Annual Grammy Awards, held at the Staples Center, Los Angeles, on February 8, 2004.

THE PUSH

IN THE WORDS OF SAM JENNINGS

"The NPG Music Club was a success. I got progressively more involved, not just in the technical stuff but with artwork, too. I decided the running order for the tracks on *The Chocolate Invasion* and *Slaughterhouse* compilations. I sat with the engineer and structured them. Prince gave me an executive producer credit.

There was some stuff that didn't come out, too. I did the artwork for *The Very Best of Prince*. I worked on a package for *The Rainbow Children Part 2* in 2003. There was an artist, Pablo Lobato, who did a picture of Prince for a newspaper. Prince liked it, so he bought the rights to the image and commissioned Pablo to make a picture of his wife, Manuela. That was going to be the cover of *The Rainbow Children 2*.

In 2004, it felt like everything lined up. With *Musicology,* he made things more accessible. It was more comfortable and less profound. He planned a polished promotional tour with the dates booked well in advance—completely different to the last minute shows he'd been playing. He just decided 'this is going to be the push.' It was a great year for the Music Club. The most successful ever. When we started it, he was a kind of underground artist. In 2004, he went mainstream again."

> INDUCTION INTO THE ROCK AND ROLL HALL OF FAME, A TAILOR-MADE ALBUM DISTRIBUTION DEAL WITH A MAJOR LABEL AND A U.S. ARENA TOUR SPANNING SEVEN MONTHS MEANS PRINCE IS THE HIGHEST-EARNING MUSICIAN OF 2004.

OUT OF HIS SYSTEM

IN THE WORDS OF MICHAEL BLAND

"Just after the *Musicology* tour, Sonny and I got called in to play with a three-piece horn section and Prince on piano. It was an early rock-and-roll, Ray Charles–style thing. It was incredible. I don't know what will happen to any of that music. None of it has come out. I think Prince did some things to get them out of his system. It wasn't for anyone else."

ABOVE Pass for the Musicology tour, March–September 2004.

OPPOSITE On stage at the 10th Anniversary Essence Music Festival, Superdome, New Orleans, July 2, 2004.

3121

IN THE WORDS OF SAM JENNINGS

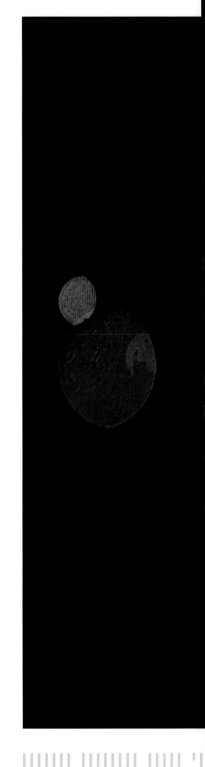

"*Musicology* meant Prince got paid. A lot. The tour was huge. The record did well. He took that cash and upgraded all the studios at Paisley Park. He rented a house in L.A. and decided to make a movie. I was being sent pictures from the set in L.A. Liza Lena, Miss Panama, was in it.

Prince's house number in West Hollywood was 3121. He started throwing house parties. At the start it was just for friends. It was a really intimate environment and Prince would play in the main room. There was no stage, so you could just walk around and talk to people. Just like he says in the song, we could 'Drink Champagne from a glass with chocolate handles'. He had 3,121 napkins and chocolates and all kinds of stuff.

Stevie Wonder came over, so naturally he sat in on keyboard. Matthew McConaughey would always play bongos. It was more about the spirit than the skill. I bumped into Jude Law. Baz Luhrmann would stand around talking to Salma Hayek. It was very Hollywood. The room was full of people who don't socialize in public places. Prince felt like these people were kind of his colleagues. He was playing for his friends.

3121 started as a physical space, but it became synonymous with a vibe. The first time I heard '3121,' it was a rock song, but the whole concept evolved. He was saying, 'You carry it with you. We are the party.' The original album cover was the 3121 house. You had to fold out the gates. One disc was *3121 The Music*. The other was *3121 The Movie*. There is a final version of the movie, but only the album made release.

He was committed. The album hit number one. He was working with a major label on his own terms and he was more willing to play the game. That's why he played the Super Bowl halftime show. To create a moment in history and to be seen. *Planet Earth* was a quicker album. There was no lyric book and the artwork didn't get a lot of revising. He said, 'Have me standing over Earth. Have some planets around it.' It was that simple."

OPPOSITE The halftime show, Super Bowl XLI, the Dolphin Stadium, Miami, February 4, 2007.

SUMMER 2007, PRINCE ANNOUNCES A RESIDENCY, "21 NIGHTS IN LONDON." TICKETS COST £31.21.

THE ACCOMPANYING ALBUM *PLANET EARTH* COMPLETES A TRILOGY OF RELEASES BACKED BY MAJOR LABELS. IT'S GIVEN TO EACH OF THE 352,000 TICKET HOLDERS AND AS A UK NEWSPAPER-COVER MOUNT.

WWW.LOTUSFLOW3R.COM

IN THE WORDS OF ANTHONY MALZONE, ART DIRECTOR, 2008 –2013

"It was winter 2008 in L.A. A colleague mentioned a possible web design project 'for a musician.' It seemed a little vague, so I assumed it was someone up-and-coming. A couple of months later, my phone beeped. My colleague texted: 'Prince says come over tonight. Can you make it?'

Inside the house there were candles everywhere. In walks Prince wearing a translucent black shirt and the most beautiful glass flower cuff links I've ever seen.

We didn't talk about the actual project for about three hours. President Obama was about to be sworn in and that was on Prince's mind. We did politics, race, and religion. He was like some kind of professor. He made my colleague and I read the same passage from three different versions of the Bible. The last one read something like, 'I am Jehovah. That is my name.' It was pretty clear he was trying to test my personality and figure me out.

At the end of the night we went into his bedroom. I remember a white furry carpet and wondering if I should take my shoes off. We listened to the first track from his new record *Lotusflow3r*. Prince explained he had three albums ready to go. He wanted me to help design a website to get them out.

A few days later, I emailed across an image I'd worked on. Almost as soon as I hit send, I got a message back: 'We have to work together.' That image became the album cover. He burned the *Lotusflow3r* album onto a CD for me to take home as a reference point for the rest of the artwork.

I heard the second album, *MPLSound*, a month later. It's a dance record. I remember showing him a drawing of a disco ball with jellyfish legs. I told him the album inspired it and the next day he played me an instrumental called 'Disco Jellyfish.' We uploaded that right away.

The site was space themed. It had so much potential. He wanted to sign other artists to have their own 'galaxy' in this virtual universe. He was releasing two albums on there and a protégé album by Bria Valente. Ultimately, it was meant to be a label, like Tidal is now. He said, 'We need to find the next Kings of Leon. We need to find the next "Sex on Fire."'

The week of release was the craziest of my life. On Tuesday, the site went live. Wednesday, Thursday, and Friday he played *Jay Leno* and on Saturday he did three shows at venues across L.A. I was with him all the way. I did the set design for Leno and made large-scale 3D disco-jellyfish to hang above the stage for the live shows.

Before he'd go onstage, the whole crew would get in a circle and give thanks. I'm not a fan of religion, but it was just a way of being positive and saying, 'Thank you for letting us do this.' His backing singer Shelby would always lead the prayer. It made us feel united. It's like getting hyped before a game, just like footballers coming out of the tunnel onto the field. I remember the band walking out first, then Prince and then me. It felt like walking out behind the captain. He went left to the stage and I walked to my seat to watch the show. It was magic. I'll never forget that for as long as I live."

OPPOSITE *On stage at Coachella Festival, Indio, California, April 26, 2008.*

LEFT Performing the first of three shows in one night at three different L.A. venues the Nokia Theatre, Los Angeles, March 28, 2009.

HE MOVED ON

IN THE WORDS OF ANTHONY MALZONE

"There was so much good intention for the website, [www.LOtUSFLOW3R.com], but by the time it went live, we'd been discussing it for three months. That's like thirty years in his world. The site kind of just stopped. He was ready to do something different. It's tough to be a Prince fan, I tell you that. He led fans on a wild journey.

By 2010, I was working as his art director. He wanted me to design the sound stage. I asked him about a theme and he said, 'Just make it weird.' Being at Paisley was a complete workout. I could never relax. Everything needed to be done yesterday. By that point, I was doing set design, decor, and even helping design his clothes. Remember those turtle necks with graphics printed on them? I did a lot of that stuff.

One morning, he said, 'Today we're designing a box set.' *20Ten* was meant to be his next big release. That silhouette on the cover with contrapposto pose came from his clothing designer. I did the colors and finished the face. The music was like a lava lamp for me. It could shape into anything. In the background, there's a figurative profile of a face with stuff dripping into its mouth. The music made that happen. I was happy to go there!

20Ten was meant to be a deluxe box set. I have a piece of artwork that goes with every song on there. I have artwork for 'Rich Friends,' too, which was meant to be a single. It never came out. Instead, he gave the album away as a cover mount. He moved on to the next thing."

ABOVE On stage at the Yas Arena, Abu Dhabi,
United Arab Emirates, November 14, 2010.

THE MOST FAMOUS MUSICIAN IN THE WORLD

IN THE WORDS OF ANDREW GOUCHÉ, BASS, 2011–2014

"I was Chaka Khan's musical director and we opened up for Prince on his Welcome 2 America tour in 2011. He came to find me backstage and said, 'Dude, you killed it! I've never heard a bass sound like that. Who did those arrangements?' I said, 'I did!'

I became a fan when I started working with him. He is a true musician. He just happened to be the most famous musician in the world. He would go to the smallest, dirtiest clubs to see a jam session and, if he felt like it, he'd jump up and join in, too.

By December 2011, I'd been called out to Paisley. It was me, Jubu Smith on guitar, Michael Bland on drums, and Cassandra O'Neal on keys. He got us to learn songs and we played together for five days. At the end of it he said, 'You're all hired!' Then the phone didn't ring for months.

Eventually, I was called back to play shows. I was the last bass player with the NPG. No one else can say that. I was by far the oldest guy in the band. I'd say, 'I have kids older than you guys!' In one of the rehearsals, some of the younger players were teasing me about my age and Prince jumped in, all stern over the mic, 'You know I'm a year older than Gouché.' It got really quiet and it took us a minute to figure out he was playing."

ABOVE *Pass for the Welcome 2 America tour, December 2010– May 2011.*

LEFT *With protégé Andy Allo on stage at the North Sea Jazz Festival, Ahoy, Rotterdam, July 10, 2011.*

OPPOSITE *On stage during the Welcome 2 America tour, Madison Square Garden, New York City, February 7, 2011.*

3RDEYETUNES

IN THE WORDS OF DAVE MEYER, WEB DESIGNER, 3RDEYEGIRL.COM, 2013

"It was February 2013. We got a call from the Prince camp saying he wanted a platform to get new content out. He didn't want people to know it was him, so the URL would be www.3rdeyegirl.com. He'd already set up a Facebook page describing 3rdEyeGirl as an 'international art thief.' He'd post snippets of unreleased music and take them down soon after. He even posted a picture of a fake cease-and-desist order suggesting the page was run by a bootlegger. But it was Prince. He understood the value of intrigue. It was completely hush-hush. He had a Twitter account that was left and right of what was really happening. It was mischievous misdirection.

The call came on a Thursday and we were told we had to go live the following Monday. The next sixty hours were wonderful and terrifying. We posted an image of the 3rdEyeGirl painting along with an audio flourish of a woman whispering, 'Shhhh.'

We had agreed a four a.m. Central Time launch and built servers to respond to traffic flow. What did Prince do? He tweeted a link ten minutes early. We had 100,000 people on the site in ten minutes. The server crashed so hard, it couldn't be rebooted.

It was stressful, but it was also tremendous fun. We were essentially building a mini iTunes® or, in this case, 3rdEyeTunes. It was mostly an experiment. He'd release a track, check the buzz, and change it the next day. There was no filter between Prince's mind and the audience."

OPPOSITE With 3rdEyeGirl at the Billboard Music Awards, the MGM Grand Arena, Las Vegas, May 19, 2013.

YOU SHOULD BE YOUR FAVORITE MUSICIAN

IN THE WORDS OF MARCUS ANDERSON, SAXOPHONE, 2012–2016

"I was doing a club show. I was approached by someone who said they represent 'a major artist.' I thought it was LA talk. You know, people do a lot of that 'Give me your number' chat. I almost made up some bogus digits. I'm glad I didn't. That was Sunday. On Wednesday I got a call. I was flown to Minneapolis and I began working with Prince in July 2012.

He wanted to create a horn section with me, Maceo Parker, and Trombone Shorty, but he changed his mind and started thinking bigger. We got an eleven-piece together. It was the biggest horn section he ever played with.

It was collaborative. I put horn lines on 'Look at Me, Look at U', '2Y2D', and 'Revelation', too. That all came out on the last album. He'd tell us what he wanted, lay it down, mix it at night when we were gone, and then play it to us the next day, finished. There are so many songs that I only got to hear once, because they never came out.

Sometimes, he'd stop a session and ask everyone a question like, 'Who is your favorite sax player?' We spoke about the greats and then the bassist said, 'Marcus is my favorite.' I laughed. You know, I'm a jazz musician from the Carolinas!

Prince jumped in, 'Why is that funny, Marcus?' He explained, 'I am my favorite on guitar. I'm my favorite on keys, and I'm my favorite drummer, too. I know what music should sound like in my head. I want to sound like me. You should be your favorite musician.'

It wasn't arrogance. He was speaking about the security of loving yourself. It made me embrace my own sound. He taught me something that day."

PREVIOUS PAGE   *On stage at the Skanderborg Festival, Denmark, August 7, 2013.*

OPPOSITE   *With his eleven-piece horn section on stage at the Hollywood Palladium, Los Angeles, March 8, 2014.*

"THERE ARE SO MANY SONGS THAT I ONLY GOT TO HEAR ONCE, BECAUSE THEY NEVER CAME OUT."

MARCUS ANDERSON

THE EGG THAT DIDN'T HATCH

IN THE WORDS OF ANDREW GOUCHÉ

" The New Power Generation Quartet was completely different from what we'd done before. He got four players in a room and left for a week. Me, Marcus Anderson on sax, Xavier Taplin on keys, and John Blackwell on drums.

I knew what was going on. He wanted us to make music, so that's what we did. He came back and asked, 'What you been doing?' We played for him on the sound stage at Paisley and he almost fell out of his chair. A few days later, we recorded the nine tracks in Studio A and he added guitar to some stuff.

Prince was getting ready to book shows for us, but the drummer, John Blackwell, left to do the D'Angelo tour. Prince shut the whole thing down and acted like it never existed. It killed it for all of us. It got weird being there after that. I'm old enough to not count my eggs before they hatch. That one didn't hatch. "

OPPOSITE *On stage at the Hollywood Palladium, Los Angeles, March 8, 2014.*

> **" IT WAS LIKE A WHIRLWIND AND IT MEANT THAT EVERY TIME I WAS THERE, I'D TRY TO TAKE IT ALL IN AND MAKE THE MOST OF THOSE MOMENTS. "**
> *MARCUS ANDERSON*

APRIL 2014, EIGHTEEN YEARS AFTER TERMINATING THE CONTRACT HE SIGNED AS A TEENAGER, PRINCE STRIKES A DEAL WITH WARNER BROTHERS RECORDS TO REGAIN OWNERSHIP OF HIS MASTER RECORDINGS. IN SEPTEMBER, HE RELEASES TWO NEW ALBUMS: *ART OFFICIAL AGE* AND HIS FIRST RECORD WITH 3RDEYEGIRL, *PLECTRUMELECTRUM*.

NEW POWER MOTOWN

IN THE WORDS OF MARCUS ANDERSON

" He was positive and optimistic and saw opportunity in everything. He wanted to establish a new-age Motown, to bring in artists and have a band ready for them to record with. We did Andy Allo's *Superconductor* album, Liv Warfield's *The Unexpected,* Judith Hill's *Back in Time,* and we were working on some stuff with Kandace Springs, too. I remember Rita Ora hanging out in the studio. There were just a whole bunch of people coming into Paisley Park.

It was like a whirlwind and it meant that every time I was there, I'd try to take it all in and make the most of those moments. We had a sense of belonging. It felt like a homecoming.

We rarely knew exactly what we were working on, but in fall 2014 he stripped down the New Power Generation band he was touring with and said, 'Now we're making a jazz album.' I cowrote 'Dandelion' with him after he told me a story about his father. He remembered being a child and picking flowers in a dandelion field. He didn't talk about that stuff often, but it stuck with me. I wrote it and he finished it off.

At the same time, he was working on a second 3rdEyeGirl record, too. There was just so much music being made: different styles, different voices, different players. "

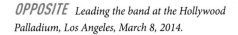

OPPOSITE Leading the band at the Hollywood Palladium, Los Angeles, March 8, 2014.

SEPTEMBER 2015, PRINCE RELEASES HITNRUN PHASE ONE. THREE MONTHS LATER, PHASE TWO COMES OUT. THESE BECOME THE FINAL ALBUM RELEASES OF PRINCE'S LIFE.

BLACK IS THE NEW BLACK

IN THE WORDS OF MONONEON, BASS, 2015–2016

"The first time I met him he said, 'I saw you before I heard you.' He was cool with my high-visibility colors and the sock on the end of my bass. I thought he'd want me to be a particular way to fit in with him, but he allowed me to be MonoNeon with no compromising.

Prince knew I didn't talk much, but he felt my vision and what I wanted to do. There were studio sessions with Kirk Johnson on drums, Adrian Crutchfield on sax, and me on bass. Prince would play keys from the control room. He would usually tell Kirk the beat, or tell us what key, but it was mostly improvised. He'd sometimes say, 'Don't overplay,' but there was a lot of freedom. He'd smile at me after I'd solo. There was a lot of obvious love. I didn't expect that and it's something I'll cherish.

We recorded nine tracks in a week, I think. We finished up in February. He told me he was calling the album *Black is the New Black*. I think it was an Afro-centric thing. It was an experimental groove record, similar to the *Madhouse* album from back in the day. It was finished. He brought in engineers to mix it. Kirk, Adrian, and me even had a photo shoot to promote 'Ruff Enuff,' the only thing that was released from the project. He went on his solo Piano and Microphone tour and I thought I would see him when he was back.

Prince gave me so much love and freedom. I didn't have to change nothing. He just let me play. It would be really cool to perhaps turn Paisley Park into some kinda music school. Keep the studios and stage rooms accessible for recording and live shows. To me that will at least keep Paisley Park vibrant and full of sound. Not just a place for nostalgia. I'm so thankful Prince embraced me and gave me a chance. I'm going to miss him dearly. "

OPPOSITE The final concert, Piano and a Microphone tour, Fox Theatre, Atlanta, April 14, 2016.

DISCOGRAPHY

1978	FOR YOU
1979	PRINCE
1980	DIRTY MIND
1981	CONTROVERSY
1982	1999
1984	PURPLE RAIN
1985	AROUND THE WORLD IN A DAY
1986	PARADE
1987	SIGN O' THE TIMES
1988	LOVESEXY
1989	BATMAN
1990	GRAFFITI BRIDGE
1991	DIAMONDS AND PEARLS
1992	♀
1993	THE HITS/THE B-SIDES
1994	COME

1994	THE BLACK ALBUM
1995	THE GOLD EXPERIENCE
1996	CHAOS AND DISORDER
1996	EMANCIPATION
1998	CRYSTAL BALL
1998	THE TRUTH
1999	THE VAULT . . . OLD FRIENDS 4 SALE
1999	RAVE UN2 THE JOY FANTASTIC
2001	RAVE IN2 THE JOY FANTASTIC
2001	THE VERY BEST OF PRINCE
2001	THE RAINBOW CHILDREN
2002	ONE NITE ALONE
2002	ONE NITE ALONE . . . LIVE!
2003	XPECTATION
2003	N.E.W.S.

EPILOGUE

A curious whirlpool spun since Prince lodged himself into our collective consciousness. Anyone with an interest in contemporary music knew there was another Prince album around the corner, and for fans, that well of purple water was a promise that there was more to be revealed. A new tour, a new concept, and, most important, new music would spill from Prince's mind and flow to us. Another piece of the puzzle to enjoy.

On April 21, 2016, the water stopped flowing. It broke the laws of physics. Nothing can occupy the space. A fairy tale of this magnitude deserves a more poetic ending, surely?

So many of the conversations I had while making this book followed a pattern. Again and again, the same sentiment was expressed, "There was unfinished business," "I always thought I'd see him again," "I assumed the phone would ring and there would be some conclusion to what we did." The question of Prince is not confined to the public space. Even his closest collaborators accept they were only ever seeing glimpses of what he was willing to reveal at that given moment.

It's about control. Everyone has a story to tell about Prince's need to govern, not only his music but as much of his world as possible. The mystery, the personas, the legend of the vault are not accidents. Michael Bland says, "Prince is a product of his own imagination." Eric Leeds is more explicit still: "He invented himself." There is a melody there, expressed over and over again.

The dichotomy of Prince's eyes seducing the world to come closer while he pulls a mask over his face is as frustrating as it is exciting. He achieved the desired outcome and then left us without finishing the sentence.

When *Hunting for Prince's Vault* was released in 2015, the documentary's top line "If Prince was to leave the world today, he has enough material to release an album a year for the next one hundred years," gained a lot of traction. There was awe but also the obvious question: why isn't this stuff coming out? Is it just another method of engineering enigma? Is he waiting for something?

With the benefit of perspective, Prince's single-minded obsession with making music was so otherworldly that the persona of Prince will always be secondary. He once said, "If I didn't make music, I'd die." It was always about the music, to the last day. Regardless of if, and how, much of his unreleased recordings come to light, Prince gave us so much music. It's beautiful. It makes the world better. Its impact will live on. In that, there is comfort and a happy ever after.

OPPOSITE On stage at the Essence Music Festival, Superdome, New Orleans, July 4, 2014.

STERLING
New York

An Imprint of Sterling Publishing Co., Inc.
1166 Avenue of the Americas
New York, NY 10036

STERLING and the distinctive Sterling logo are registered trademarks of Sterling Publishing Co., Inc.

Text © 2016 by Mobeen Azhar

All rights reserved. No part of this publication may be reproduced, stored in a retrieval system, or transmitted in any form or by any means (including electronic, mechanical, photocopying, recording, or otherwise) without prior written permission from the publisher.

This book is an independent publication and is not associated with or authorized, licensed, sponsored or endorsed by any person, entity or product affiliated with Prince or his music. All trademarks are the property of their respective owners, are used for editorial purposes only, and the publisher makes no claim of ownership and shall acquire no right, title, or interest in such trademarks by virtue of this publication.

ISBN 978-1-4549-2246-9

Distributed in Canada by Sterling Publishing
c/o Canadian Manda Group, 664 Annette Street
Toronto, Ontario, Canada M6S 2C8

For information about custom editions, special sales, and premium and corporate purchases, please contact Sterling Special Sales at 800-805-5489 or specialsales@sterlingpublishing.com.

Manufactured in China

1 3 5 7 9 10 8 6 4 2

www.sterlingpublishing.com

Design by Carlton Books Limited

CREDITS

The publishers would like to thank the following sources for their kind permission to reproduce the pictures in this book.
2. © Rob Verhorst/Redferns/Getty Images, 4–5. © Robert Whitman/thelicensingproject.com, 6. © Retna/Photoshot, 9. © Robert Whitman/thelicensingproject.com, 11. & 12. © Larry Falk, 13. © Robert Whitman/thelicensingproject.com, 14–15. © Larry Falk, 16. © Heidi Suzanne Melick, 18. (top) © Bruce Kessler/RockinHouston.com, 18. (bottom) © Alan Singer/NBC/NBCU Photo Bank/Getty Images, 19. © Bruce Kessler/RockinHouston.com, 20–21. © Allen Beaulieu, 22. © Waring Abbott/Getty Images, 23. © Bruce Kessler/RockinHouston.com, 24–25. © Waring Abbott/Michael Ochs Archives/Getty Images, 27 & 29. © Allen Beaulieu, 30. © Paul Natkin/WireImage/Getty Images, 31. (left) © Ron Galella, Ltd./WireImage/Getty Images, 31. (right) © Bruce Kessler/RockinHouston.com, 32. © Michael Ochs Archives/Getty Images, 33. © Paul Natkin/WireImage/Getty Images, 35. © The LIFE Picture Collection/Getty Images, 36. © Bruce Kessler/RockinHouston.com, 39. © Everett/REX/Shutterstock, 40. © Michael Putland/Getty Images, 42–43. © GEMA Images/IconicPix, 44–45. © Roger Ressmeyer/Corbis/VCG via Getty Images, 47. © Press Association Images, 48. © Bruce Kessler/RockinHouston.com, 49. © Jim Steinfeldt/Michael Ochs Archives/Getty Images, 51 & 52. © Rob Verhorst/Redferns/Getty Images, 53. © Bruce Kessler/RockinHouston.com, 54. © Bertrand Guay/AFP/Getty Images, 56–57. © Rob Verhorst/Redferns/Getty Images, 58. © Scanpix/Press Association Images, 60. © Mirrorpix, 61. Stephen Wright/Premium Archive/Getty Images, 62. © Michael Putland/Getty Images, 63. © Bruce Kessler/RockinHouston.com, 64–65. © ZUMA Press, Inc./Alamy Stock Photo, 67. © Rob Verhorst/Redferns/Getty Images, 68. © Michel Linssen/Redferns/Getty Images, 71. © Rob Verhorst/Redferns/Getty Images, 72. © Mirrorpix, 75. © Paul Bergen/Redferns/Getty Images, 76–77. © Rob Verhorst/Redferns/Getty Images, 79. © Tim Rooke/REX/Shutterstock, 80–81. © The LIFE Picture Collection/Getty Images, 85. © Tim Dickson/REX/Shutterstock, 86. © Paul Bergen/Redferns/Getty Images, 87. © Craig Blankenhorn/NBC/NBCU Photo Bank via Getty Images, 89. © Courtesy of Elizabeth Van Huffel, 91. © Tony Bock/Toronto Star via Getty Images, 92. © Steve Eichner/Getty Images, 93. (left) © Tim Mosenfelder/ImageDirect/Getty Images, 93. (right) © Bruce Kessler/RockinHouston.com, 94–95. © Bob Berg/Getty Images, 96. © AP/Press Association Images, 97. © LFI/Photoshot, 98. © Steve Parke, 99. © Ebet Roberts/Redferns/Getty Images, 100–110. © Steve Parke, 112. © Paul Drinkwater/NBC/NBCU Photo Bank via Getty Images, 113. © Bruce Kessler/RockinHouston.com, 115. © Frank Micelotta/Getty Images, 116. © Bruce Kessler/RockinHouston.com, 117. © Chris Graythen/Getty Images, 119. © Jamie Squire/Getty Images, 120. © Spencer Weiner/Los Angeles Times/Contour by Getty Images, 122–123. © Kristian Dowling/Getty Images for Lotusflow3r.com, 124–125. © Retna/Photoshot, 126. (left) © Brian Ach/WireImage for NPG Records 2011/Getty Images, 126. (right) © Bruce Kessler/RockinHouston.com, 127. © Kevin Mazur/WireImage for NPG Records 2011/Getty Images, 129. © Kevin Mazur/WireImage/Getty Images, 130–131. © PYMCA/UIG via Getty Images, 133–136. © Kevin Mazur/WireImage for NPG Records 2013/Getty Images, 139. © Evan Carter Photography/evancarterphotography.com, 142–143. © NPG Records/REX

Special thank you to Allen Beaulieu, Thomas de Bruin, George Chin, Larry Falk, Bruce Kessler, Heidi Suzanne Melick and Steve Parke for their help on this book.